The Forest Fights Back

The Forest Fights Back

A Global Movement for the Rights of Nature

Jessica den Outer

PLUTO PRESS

First English language edition published 2026 by Pluto Press
New Wing, Somerset House, Strand, London WC2R 1LA
and Pluto Press, Inc.
1930 Village Center Circle, 3-834, Las Vegas, NV 89134

www.plutobooks.com

This book was originally published in Dutch with the title *Rechten voor de Natuur* (Uitgeverij Lemniscaat, 2023). It was meant as a plea for the recognition of the Rights of Nature in the Netherlands. Some parts are adapted or left out in this English translation, as they were specifically focused on the situation in the Netherlands.

British Library Cataloguing in Publication Data
A catalogue record for this book is available from the British Library

ISBN 978 0 7453 5148 3   Paperback
ISBN 978 0 7453 5150 6   PDF
ISBN 978 0 7453 5149 0   EPUB

This book is printed on paper suitable for recycling and made from fully managed and sustained forest sources. Logging, pulping and manufacturing processes are expected to conform to the environmental standards of the country of origin.

Typeset by Stanford DTP Services, Northampton, England

Simultaneously printed in the United Kingdom and United States of America

EU GPSR Authorised Representative
LOGOS EUROPE, 9 rue Nicolas Poussin, 17000, LA ROCHELLE, France
Email: Contact@logoseurope.eu

Nature, or Pacha Mama [Mother Earth], where life is reproduced and occurs, has the right to integral respect for its existence and for the maintenance and regeneration of its life cycles, structure, functions and evolutionary processes.

All persons, communities, peoples, and nations can call upon public authorities to enforce the rights of nature. To enforce and interpret these rights, the principles set forth in the Constitution shall be observed, as appropriate.

The State shall give incentives to natural persons, and legal entities and to communities to protect nature and to promote respect for all the elements comprising an ecosystem.

Constitution of Ecuador 2008, Article 71

I dedicate this book to my grandfather (†), who inspired me at a young age to explore the mysteries of nature and to pass that fascination on to others. I also dedicate this book to the rolling hills and moors in Yorkshire, where we scattered my grandfather's ashes.

Contents

Introduction

An ecocentric approach to the law

For centuries, humans have placed themselves at the centre of everything, including our legal systems. The law has treated nature as an object, something that humans can use, own and exploit for their own gain. But that paradigm is shifting. In recent decades, more and more legal systems around the world have begun to recognise the Rights of Nature. The question is no longer *whether* Nature has rights, but *when* the rest of the world will follow, by recognising Nature's rights to exist, thrive and evolve. In 2024, the *Guardian* published an article headed 'Could 2024 be the year nature rights enter the political mainstream?' following the growing worldwide movement for the Rights of Nature.[1]

Nowadays, hardly anyone would deny that our survival depends on the nature around us: trees provide oxygen, bees pollinate crops, and algae in the ocean stabilise the climate. Yet people pollute and destroy the Earth, as if the future is of no concern. Areas of rainforest the size of football pitches vanish daily. Rivers are full of microplastics. The CEOs of companies responsible for ecological destruction rarely face accountability.

This is not just a moral failure, but a legal one too. The anthropocentric nature of laws and policies is obvious: humankind, as the centre of existence, is the starting point of laws and regulations. Laws were designed to regulate human activity, not to protect the integrity of ecosystems. Nature's intrinsic value is barely recognised. Economic interests weigh more heavily than ecological ones.

But things could be different. We can turn the tide by changing the law. It is of utmost importance that we adopt a new way of thinking and acting towards the rest of nature (that is, humans are part of nature, hence besides human rights there need to be rights for the rest of nature). In an era defined by climate change, biodiversity loss, and other ecological crises, we simply cannot afford to carry on as before.

We must shift towards an ecocentric approach, where the wellbeing of the entire Earth community is at the heart of decision-making. Not just humans but the entire ecosystem should be the starting point of laws and regulations. The time has come for the legal emancipation of nature, by recognising that just as humans have a right to life on this planet, forests, rivers, and mountains do too.

A river as a legal person

I have always been fascinated by nature. When I was a little girl, my grandfather would often take me out into our garden to explore. On hands and knees, we would crawl through the grass and study all the little creatures swarming, buzzing, and zooming through it. Discovering the wonderful world of insects was, and still is, a big adventure to me. In this small back garden, my great love for nature was born. During my teenage years I started to work as a volunteer and decided to go to law school because I was looking for a way to express my natural sense of justice. When I took a course in environmental law, I realised that in this field, I could combine my love for nature and my interest in the law. I decided to specialise in environmental law. I learned about all the legal regulations, conventions, and legal measures that countries take to protect the environment.

As I memorised dozens of laws and regulations on conservation and climate change, I kept hearing on the news about how badly things were going for the planet. The number of alarming scientific reports on the effects of global warming and the disappearance of animal and plant species kept increasing. How was this possible, when there are countless laws and regulations aimed at protecting nature, I asked myself? That got me thinking: I want to use my legal knowledge to investigate how things might be done differently. I did not want to remain stuck in an outdated legal system, which clearly is not working.

In 2017, I read an article in the newspaper about the legal personality of the Whanganui River in Aotearoa/New Zealand. For the first time ever, a river had been recognised as a legal person. Filled with disbelief, I read the article. At university, I had learned that certain corporate forms, organisations, and governmental institutions could have legal personality. But I had never heard of a forest, river, or mountain becoming a legal person. I was intrigued. As it turned out, Aotearoa/New Zealand was not the first country to assign this legal status to nature. Other countries, such as Ecuador and Bolivia, had previously recognised the rights of Mother Earth. My fascination with this new form of nature protection was born.

When it was time to write my thesis, I knew I wanted to write about this legal innovation. Whereas my fellow law students focused on existing laws and regulations, I decided to take a risk and immerse myself in an unfamiliar development in the law. I began my thesis research on the Rights of Nature and discovered that a distorted worldview underpins our legal systems. Humans, especially in the West, are seen as rulers over the rest of nature. This belief is reflected in the legal position of nature. Nature and all its components are seen as objects without rights, which we can possess, exhaust, and use for our own benefit.

The Rights of Nature is a legal and philosophical concept that maintains that nature has inherent rights, just like humans. In this line of reasoning, nature is a subject of rights, rather than an object without rights. The Universal Declaration of Human Rights states that every human being has the right to life, education, and freedom of expression. These rights must be upheld regardless of how others perceive one's value. The rest of nature also has fundamental rights to what is necessary to preserve and respect Earth's cycles, structure, functions, and evolutionary processes. Long before humans existed, nature lived, thrived, and evolved. We are only just now beginning to recognise and embed these rights in legal systems. That is why we are not talking about granting but rather *recognising* the Rights of Nature. By doing so, we recognise that nature has intrinsic value, not because it means something to humans, nor because it is important for human survival, but for its own sake. This reminds me of Alice Walker's quote: animals were not made for humans any more than black people were made for white people, or women created for men. Recognising the Rights of Nature enables us to change our worldview and ensure justice for the rest of nature. It is not a silver bullet and the only solution to the ecological crisis, but it is one of the first steps that we can take, right now.

The fastest growing legal movement of the twenty-first century

The roots of the Rights of Nature stretch back some 54 years. In 1972, the foundations for the Rights of Nature were laid by jurists, the most famous of whom was Christopher D. Stone following publication of his article 'Should Trees Have Standing? Towards Legal Rights for Natural Objects'.[2] At the time, the Rights of Nature concept was portrayed as a romantic idea, but today it is much more than that. According to the Eco Jurisprudence Monitor, there are as many as 552 initiatives worldwide aimed at recognising Rights of Nature, with over 70 per cent approved.[3] Around 40 countries have enshrined Rights of Nature in laws and regulations. Think of the legal personality of a river, mountain and forest in Aotearoa/New Zealand, or the rights of Mother Earth in Ecuador's Constitution. The United Nations Secretary General has called Earth Jurisprudence, the underlying philosophy of the Rights of Nature, 'the fastest growing (legal) movement of the twenty-first century'.[4] Changes are happening incredibly fast. While I was writing this book, I regularly had to amend paragraphs to reflect the latest developments.

My thesis on Rights of Nature in 2017 was just the beginning. While researching, I became involved with the United Nations Harmony with Nature programme. This programme works to contribute to the United Nations Sustainable Development Goal 12.8: by 2030, we must ensure that all people have relevant information about – and are aware of – sustainable development and lifestyles in harmony with nature.

When I finished my thesis, I continued to spend evenings and weekends researching the countries that have recognised the Rights of Nature. I was intrigued and could not let go. From the Rights of Nature in Ecuador to India to the United States, there were so many stories of local heroes standing up for the legal emancipation of nature. Coming from a legal background, I quickly found I had to immerse myself in philosophy, theology, anthropology, and other fields to fully grasp and understand the Rights of Nature. It is much more than a legal concept, and that is why it is groundbreaking and potentially transformative.

I was surprised to find that hardly anyone in my home country, the Netherlands, knew about this global movement. Just a couple of jurists and artists were researching the Rights of Nature, and an Embassy of the North Sea was formed, but the general public did not know about the global Rights of Nature advances that were taking place. I decided to use my voice and began to advocate for the Rights of Nature in the Netherlands. The Embassy of the North Sea was founded in 2018 and aims to represent the plants, animals, microbes, and people in and around the North Sea.

Nature is not only seriously threatened in faraway countries: in the Netherlands, where everything seemingly is well organised, native biodiversity, water quality, and nature in general is under serious threat. In collaboration with a clean-up organisation called the Maas Cleanup, I started to advocate for legal personality for the Meuse River. Called 'Mother Meuse' in Limburg, a southern province in the Netherlands, the Meuse River runs through France, Belgium, and the Netherlands. In the Netherlands, the river is mockingly called the 'drain of Europe', since it is heavily polluted with industrial discharges, agricultural run-off and (micro)plastics. Together with lawyers, I decided to research permits in the

Netherlands for companies to discharge industrial chemicals into the river. How was it possible these permits were deemed legally valid? We found that while the interests of the environment must be 'taken into account' when reviewing these types of permits, societal and economic interests also factor into the equation. It happens quite often that business people and politicians conclude that human interests outweigh those of the rest of nature. The latter lack representation, while clever lawyers representing the companies know full well how to emphasise the importance of economic interests. Who represents the interests of nature in this process? Who speaks up on behalf of the fish, frogs, birds, insects, and other inhabitants of the river? Do we even take into consideration that this river and its biodiversity have rights to a clean and healthy environment? These were questions I kept asking while reviewing different kinds of permits and environmental policies. And, when corresponding with my international Rights of Nature colleagues, it seemed this situation was happening all over the world as local activists and lawyers confirmed they had similar experiences, even though our legal systems are miles apart. Nature is not recognised as a stakeholder and is undermined in many governance and permit processes. That is why, together with local activists, companies and legal professionals, we started a rights of rivers petition for the Meuse River with over 10,000 signatures. In 2026, there are now around 30 Rights of Nature initiatives in the Netherlands.[5]

Even though I had to look for a job after I graduated, I used all of my free time to share the stories of the Rights of Nature and continued to research, advise on, and advocate for the Rights of Nature. In autumn 2019, my biggest dream came true: the United Nations Harmony with Nature programme appointed me as one of the youngest experts in the field. That is when I decided to make the Rights of Nature my life's mission.

A journey around the world

This book was born out of a desire to introduce a broad group of readers to the Rights of Nature, beyond legal texts and academic journals. Many brilliant articles and books have been written about the Rights of Nature, but I found most to be focused on legal theory. The stories described in this book illustrate that the Rights of Nature is not just for lawyers. The global movement is made up of all kinds of concerned citizens, Indigenous peoples, environmental organisations, and politicians.

This book is a journey through the stories behind the Rights of Nature movement. Each chapter dives into a specific place and time where people have stood up – sometimes successfully, often against the odds – to defend the rights of ecosystems. These are not abstract legal texts. They are living stories of rivers, mountains, wetlands, and forests that have become central characters in legal and cultural battles for protection. Using examples from around the world, I try to paint a realistic picture of the opportunities, as well as the challenges, facing this movement. I want to share those stories because the Rights of Nature is not just a legal innovation but a cultural one. And culture brings about change through storytelling.

We start at a Californian sub-alpine glacial valley and travel through the United States, Aotearoa/New Zealand, India, Colombia, and Ecuador, to Spain, where a citizen's movement with 639,826 supporters led to the recognition of rights for a severely polluted saltwater lagoon, the Mar Menor. We end our journey in Sussex, England, to highlight a local success of the growing rights-of-rivers movement in the United Kingdom. Despite the many stories told in this book, the Rights of Nature movement is just getting started. It needs voices. It needs stories. It needs you. I hope you become inspired and feel compelled – like the heroes in this book – to stand up for the Rights of Nature.

Professor Stone and the birth of the Rights of Nature

Disney's attempt at a ski resort

What began as a local struggle to save a pristine wilderness sparked a legal and philosophical debate, leading to a global movement for the Rights of Nature. In the state of California in the United States, right next to the famous Sequoia National Park, lies the sub-alpine glacial valley Mineral King. It is a beautiful natural area, with thick forests, babbling brooks, and serene lakes. The names of the lakes speak for themselves: Crystal Lake, Eagle Lake, and Mosquito Lake. No modern roads or large parking lots are to be found here. Anyone wanting to visit the glacial valley can only get there via a long track leading right through the wilderness. Hikers and campers love this special place where they find peace and quiet.

In 1965, the United States Forest Service, a federal agency that manages national forests and grasslands, announced that private developers could place a bid on the valley for recreational development purposes. It seemed like a lucrative plan. The thickly snow-covered, mountainous area of Mineral King seemed perfectly suited for the construction of a huge ski resort. This news came as a complete surprise. The local community and its regular visitors reacted with disbelief. How could such a pristine wilderness be subjected to the highest bidder, bulldozers, and commercialisation?

Several parties saw an opportunity to develop a beautiful and profitable ski area at Mineral King. They expressed interest but were unable to bid enough for the glacial valley. Earlier attempts by private developers had faltered, mostly due to financial constraints and logistical challenges. Then the Walt Disney Company, Inc. came up with an offer of US $35 million. With that investment, the glacial valley would become a world-class ski resort, Disney promised, with room for more than a million visitors a year. Mineral King would be the perfect place for Disney's plans for ski elevators, big hotels, cinemas, restaurants, and parking – a true winter sports paradise.[1]

Since Mineral King could only be reached via an unpaved road running through the wilderness, a substantial highway and power grid would have to be built. The fact that more than 6 million cubic yards of stone and soil had to be cleared – destroying wildlife habitats and fragile ecosystems – seemed to be a mere afterthought in Disney's plans.

This was not the first time that nature in Mineral King had suffered at the hands of humans. The area was named Mineral King for a reason. Long before Disney came up with its grand plans for a ski resort, parts of the valley had already been excavated by silver and gold prospectors. These fortune seekers left behind traces of mining activity that altered parts of the landscape as they extracted these lucrative metals from the ground.

Although Mineral King lies near the Sequoia National Park, the resort plans did not directly threaten the giant sequoias but would disrupt vulnerable habitats and wildlife. This is an ancient landscape. Giant sequoias are among the top ten largest trees in the world, and the heaviest tree species known. They are the oldest inhabitants of California and are sometimes referred to as 'living dinosaurs'. Standing at the foot of these towering giants, visitors often feel humbled. The oldest trees are up to 2,000 years old. Their thick bark and tall crown protect the giant sequoias from the wildfires that are a regular occurrence in California. This is one of the special features that allows these trees to live so long and grow so large.

Giant sequoia trees may have it tougher now than ever before. They have a protected status but face various threats. That is partly because of the increasing intensity and frequency of forest fires, resulting from climate change. It does not help that the trees reproduce incredibly slowly. Their seeds are housed in a kind of pinecone that only opens during periods of extreme drought. It can take a very long time until the right conditions occur for the seeds to germinate.[2]

Environmental organisation in action

The Sierra Club, founded in 1892, is one of the largest and most well-known environmental organisations in the United States. These passionate environmentalists followed the development of plans for Mineral King closely and sprang into action when Disney announced its plans. They turned to the administrator for the area: the National Park Service. This organisation was responsible for approving the construction of the wide highway through the wilderness that had to be built for the ski resort. They tried to persuade the National

Park Service to prohibit the construction of the highway but could not convince them. The supervisor of the National Park Service, Interior Secretary Stewart Udall, approved the plans for the highway.

When this happened, the Sierra Club did not give up and decided to take legal action. In 1969, the environmentalists went to a Northern California district court with the request to protect Mineral King from Disney's destructive plans. They sued Rogers Morton, then Secretary of the Interior (hence the case name *Sierra Club v. Morton*).

In the *Sierra Club v. Morton* court case, the Sierra Club argued that the highway leading to the ski resort, which would cut across Sequoia National Park, was illegal. The road would be built at the expense of the soil, trees, and natural landscape. The government would not be able to adequately protect the wilderness if a busy road were to run right through it. This lawsuit was the beginning of a long and complicated legal battle, the consequences of which even the environmentalists could not have foreseen.

The first judge on the case issued a 'preliminary injunction', stating that the plans should be put on hold until there was more clarity in the case – a win for the Sierra Club, but unfortunately that was not the end. Documents provided by the Sierra Club stated that it had filed the lawsuit as an 'interested party', based on a specific section of the law. Section 10 of the Administrative Procedure Act states that you may bring a case if you are wronged as a person by the actions of an agency, or if you are otherwise affected or aggrieved by those actions. However, in the case against Disney, the Sierra Club was not defending its own interests, but the public interest. The Sierra Club believed that Disney's plans needed to be stopped to protect the precious nature and ecological value of Mineral King. But according to the government, the Sierra Club had no authority whatsoever to represent nature's interests in court, because you could only bring a case if you had a *personal* interest in doing so. It was argued that the Sierra Club had no *legal standing*, which refers to the legal ability of a party to start a lawsuit or participate in court proceedings.[3]

The government's argument against the Sierra Club was effective. The government appealed the district court decision, and when the Sierra Club appeared in court again, before the Ninth Circuit Court of Appeals, things did not end so well. The judges overturned the earlier ruling, concluding this time that the Sierra Club had no jurisdiction to appear in court because the environmental organisation's individuals would not *themselves* be negatively affected by the construction of the ski resort.

The Sierra Club did not back down and filed a petition for a writ of *certiorari*. In this legal action, a party asks for a review of a lower court's judicial findings in a case. The environmentalists took the matter to the United States Supreme Court, the highest court in the United States. But the Supreme Court also ruled against them. One of the judges reiterated the argument that if you want to file a lawsuit, you yourself must be directly impacted by someone else's doing. The lawsuit could be filed by hikers or campers, for example, because they could be personally affected by Disney's plans when camping. The court considered how a ski resort might inconvenience humans enjoying recreational activities, yet said nothing of the forest's wildlife, the fragile ecosystems, or the land itself. Nature had no voice and was completely sidelined by this ruling. The court system could only decide on human interests.

'Odd, frightening or laughable'

Around the time of the Supreme Court ruling, an article by Christopher D. Stone appeared in a legal journal, the *Southern California Law Review*. Stone was a professor at the University of Southern California's law school, where he taught property law and international environmental law, among other subjects. Because of his commitment to environmental law, he has been called 'the father of environmental law'. In one of his lectures, he addressed how the law had evolved over the years. Initially, we did not grant rights to the vulnerable in our society, he argued. Children, for example, long had to do without rights. Parents (and in reality, only the father) used to have control over their children's life. Women and enslaved people were also not considered 'persons' according to the law for a long time. With the recognition of rights for new groups in mind, Stone asked: why doesn't nature have rights? Stone's questions were groundbreaking in that they challenged centuries of established legal thought where nature is seen as nothing other than an object.

After his lecture, it is said that Stone searched the library for an ongoing court case in which the hypothetical Rights of Nature could potentially influence the outcome.[4] He found what he was looking for in the *Sierra Club v. Morton* case. In the article he wrote subsequently, 'Should Trees Have Standing?', he argued for the Rights of Nature: 'I am quite seriously proposing, in other words, that we give legal rights to forests, oceans, rivers, and other so-called "natural objects" in the environment – indeed, to the natural environment as a whole', he wrote. It must have sounded bizarre that first time, but that was true, according to Stone, every time the rights of a new group were brought up. It would always be 'odd, frightening or laughable' at first. After all, we find it hard to imagine that something without rights would suddenly have rights of its own. According to Stone, 'Throughout legal history, each successive extension of rights to some new entity has been, therefore, a bit unthinkable.' It takes time and struggle before the rights of a new group are recognised in law. Once, it was considered normal that human beings could be bought, sold, and owned as property. It would be unthinkable during that time that enslaved people would have rights of their own and would no longer be owned by slave owners. Women were long regarded by politicians and legal systems as too emotional, irrational, or unfit to have (voting) rights of their own. Sigmund Freud's famous quote reflects the sentiment: 'We must not allow ourselves to be deflected by the feminists who are anxious to force us to regard the two sexes as completely equal in position and worth.' Nowadays, even though women's rights are not always respected, they are embedded in international conventions and national laws.

On top of that, Stone argued, our legal system is only concerned with human interests. As an example, he cited a hypothetical case about a polluted stream. The people who live along the banks of the stream could take the polluter of the stream to court and seek damages. The judge will weigh the economic interests against the pollution, but the interests of the stream and the animals surrounding the stream are not included in that equation. They cannot claim restoration or compensation. No one speaks for the fish, insects, birds, and other wildlife around the creek. People are compensated and we lose sight of nature itself.

Therefore, Stone argued that the Rights of Nature could be represented by a legally recognised guardian. A guardian that has legal authority to represent nature and, if necessary, to bring a lawsuit on nature's behalf. The fact that streams and forests cannot talk is not a valid argument against the Rights of Nature. Corporations, government agencies, municipalities and universities also cannot speak. Yet their interests are advocated for by lawyers. Guardianship is a construct that exists for minors and the mentally ill. Guardians stand up for children's interests because they cannot properly defend themselves. But the fact that minors cannot mount their own defence does not mean that they have no rights. On the contrary: their inability to represent themselves is precisely why the legal system provides them with representation. We can apply this system to nature too. If the judges in the Sierra Club case were to recognise the Rights of Nature, it might alter human consciousness quite a bit, Stone wrote. Then we would have to start thinking about the interests of nature itself. While it would be a modest first step, it would be one in furtherance of a greater goal: the future of the planet.

An outdated worldview

If we want to leave the path of destruction of nature, we need a worldview in which humans assume a balanced role on Earth with corresponding duties and responsibilities to stand up for those that lack a human voice. Our worldview has changed fundamentally over the centuries. Especially in the West, humans have grown increasingly distant from nature, and this history goes back to the great thinkers who helped shape our societies. The Greek philosopher Aristotle, for example, stated that plants exist for animals, and animals exist for humans. Nature makes nothing that is of no use to anyone, he concluded. So, everything exists for the sake of the other. His ideas influenced the establishment of the *scala naturæ*, a hierarchical ladder of everything that lives. Humans are high on the ladder. Below us are animals, plants, and 'inanimate' things such as earth and water.

The Judeo-Christian creation story (Genesis 1) also states that God created humans to 'rule over the fish of the sea and the birds in the sky and every creature that crawls upon the earth', and commands them to 'fill the earth and subdue it' (Genesis 1:28).[5] While these verses have historically been interpreted to mean human dominance over nature, a growing number of theologians argue that its original meaning – which was not one of dominance – was lost in interpretation. Other biblical passages, including Genesis 2:15, describe the beauty and value of nature, and humans' role as one of tending and safeguarding creation.

In the late sixteenth and early seventeenth century, the English philosopher Francis Bacon also concluded that humans clearly stand above the rest of nature. Our job, he wrote, is to study nature properly so that we can develop the right technology to master it. We can use nature to achieve our goals. It appears that Bacon eventually died of pneumonia after he stuffed a dead chicken with snow to find out if that would allow the meat to be kept longer. It seems that nature still got the better of him in the end.[6]

These kinds of ideas about humans' position in relation to the rest of nature have also found their way into our legal systems. In 1972, the first United Nations Global Conference on the Human Environment was held in Stockholm. In their report, the representatives of the participating countries declared that Man is both creator and distorter of the environment.[7] The rate at which the human population has been growing since the Industrial Revolution clearly cannot be sustained, they said. And, with the progress in science and technology, humans are now able to alter the Earth's ecosystem in dramatic and negative ways.

Even though this conference finally drew attention to the environment, discussions once again revolved around human interests. This is already evident in the title of the conference which specifically mentions the human environment. Academics have strongly criticised the conference, writing that humans were solely concerned with protecting the environment for themselves and their future, and not for the rest of nature, such as flora and fauna.[8]

Because we created the law with only ourselves in mind, it is not surprising that the rest of nature has no rights. In our current legal system, a tree has the same rights as a lamppost and a crow has the same rights as a teapot. None, in other words. Humans can own or appropriate living creatures and ecosystems as they wish.

The idea of land as property took shape in the late seventeenth century in the work of British philosopher and political theorist John Locke. He believed that a piece of land can become property as soon as it is worked on by a human. By performing labour, we become entitled to everything the land provides. Today, you do not even have to work to own land: if you can pay the price, the land is yours. The Earth is literally for sale.

Mineral King v. Morton

Back to the Sierra Club case. One of the Supreme Court judges, William O. Douglas, read Stone's article. It got him thinking so much that he wrote a 'dissenting opinion' on the Supreme Court's ruling. A dissenting opinion gives you, as a judge, the opportunity to voice your own minority opinion as opposed to the opinion of the majority of the judges. Douglas, known for his environmental advocacy and progressive opinions, disagreed with the Supreme Court ruling and felt that representation of the natural entity at stake was necessary. As far as he was concerned, the case should have been called *Mineral King v. Morton*, rather than *Sierra Club v. Morton*. At least then the main stakeholder – in this case the sub-alpine glacial valley Mineral King – would have been able to participate and be heard in the case.

Judge Douglas was clearly inspired by Stone's argument. If ships and corporations can have legal personality, when in fact they are man-made 'fictions', why would a river, with all the life it sustains and feeds, not have it as well? Why not the fish, insects, birds, otters, deer, and all other animals? The river should speak as a plaintiff on behalf of the values of all life in and around the water. Similarly, anyone who has a meaningful relationship with the river (a fisherman or a canoeist, for example) must be able to speak not only for themselves, but also for the river and its values when it is threatened. 'The river as plaintiff speaks for the ecological unit of life that is part of it.'⁹

This is an important point. Later we will see Stone's proposal implemented in some countries, where specific guardians for nature have been appointed. In other countries, local citizens are empowered, in the spirit of Douglas, to stand up for the Rights of Nature.

Exactly as Stone had predicted, Douglas was told that his dissent was 'odd, frightening, or laughable'. A legal journal, the *American Bar Association Journal*, featured a mocking poem by a lawyer from which I quote an excerpt:

Great mountain peaks of names prestigious
Will suddenly become litigious.
Our brooks will babble in the courts,
Seeking damages for torts.
How can I rest beneath a tree
If it may soon be suing me?
Ah! But Vengeance will be sweet
Since this must be a two-way street.
I'll promptly sue my neighbor's tree
For shedding all its leaves on me.[10]

Judge Douglas's dissenting opinion did not and could not help the Sierra Club's plea. The Supreme Court's ruling was final: the services involved were allowed to build a highway right through the pristine wilderness for the benefit of the Disney ski resort.

In 1970, while the lawsuits were still ongoing, President Richard Nixon signed the National Environmental Policy Act, a law that required federal agencies to prepare environmental impact statements before reviewing any plan that might affect wildlife. This law was not a direct result of the lawsuit, but its mandatory environmental reviews influenced the fate of this project. For Mineral King, this change in the law came in the nick of time. Because of the new law, Disney had to postpone construction of the ski resort until the environmental impacts of its plans had been assessed. When the Forest Service's 600-page report came out six years later, Disney was no longer interested in 'a world-class ski resort' and all plans were halted. Disney probably realised the huge impact the ski resort would have on the area and considered it unlikely the plans would be approved. They cancelled the project.

Mineral King became part of Sequoia National Park in 1978, giving the area protected status.[11] You can still only get there via the long track running right through the wilderness. The giant sequoias are given the space and time they need to exist and grow, even though they are still seriously threatened by the effects of climate change. The Sierra Club is still involved in the park and in 2023 organised a trip for backpackers right through the area, highlighting the history of Mineral King and the impact the lawsuit has had on the environmental movement.

Global awareness

In the same year Stone's article was published, global awareness about the state of the environment was also growing. The illustrious Club of Rome report was published in 1972, in which scientists warned about the effects of human behaviour on the environment. There are 'limits to growth', they said. Unchecked human activities would inevitably lead to ecological collapse – a prediction we now see unfolding around us. And the scientists continued to warn of the same thing, year after year, again and again. Yet in all these years, very little has happened to protect the Earth from human activities. In not much more than a century, humans have destroyed much of the rest of nature – that is, the natural systems and environments that have taken millions of years to evolve.

You can even see the traces of destruction from outer space. André Kuipers said of his experiences as an astronaut:

> Once the clouds are gone over the Amazon rainforest, you can see in several places a light green castellated structure in the dark green: cleared rainforest along roadways, partly as a result of cattle ranching. Smoke plumes from deforestation and the fertile soil is flowing away due to erosion, as a result of forest clearing. This happens not only in the Amazon, but also in Borneo, Sumatra, Africa, and Madagascar.[12]

You do not necessarily have to look down at Earth from outer space to see the consequences of human activity. The ice caps are melting at an alarming rate, oceans are choking with plastic, and smog covers major cities like a thick blanket. Humankind's negative impact on the Earth is now so great that some believe it has ushered in a new geological era: the Anthropocene. This is derived from the word *anthropos*, meaning *human* in Greek. It is the geological epoch defined by the negative impacts of human activities.

Ancient worldviews

The laws of the Earth should determine the way we organise our legal system, according to American historian Thomas Berry. We must move away from anthropocentric thinking in which humans are a central focus, towards a new form of eco-centric thinking in which the entire ecosystem is the starting point. Indigenous peoples are already aware of this, Berry discovered. Their systems are deeply rooted in the realisation that nature regulates the order of life. They know that humans are only a (small) part of that.

According to Dutch ecologist and philosopher Matthijs Schouten, building on the ideas of French philosopher Michel Serres, two specific steps are needed to turn the tide. First, we must begin to relate differently to the rest of nature. Second, we must enshrine that awareness in a new contract. Just as human society is defined by a social contract, so too must we establish a new contract with the rest of nature that better incorporates its interests. We can do this by recognising the Rights of Nature and establishing a voice for nature. It is a first step toward a different worldview – one in which humans are part of the rest of nature and have a responsibility to stand up for the interests of rivers, forests, and mountains.

Although Stone's article and Judge Douglas's dissenting opinion could not change the ruling in *Sierra Club v. Morton*, the two jurists did lay a solid foundation for the development of the Rights of Nature. At the same time, we need to recognise that this kind of thinking is not new. Indigenous peoples inform and inspire the Rights of Nature movement with their worldviews and views on the relationship of humans to the rest of nature. The Earth Law Center discovered that the Navajo people had the Rights of Nature written in their 2002 Diné Fundamental Laws: 'All creation, from Mother Earth and Father Sky to the animals, those who live in water, those who fly and plant life have their own laws and have rights and freedoms to exist' and: 'The Diné have the sacred obligation and duty to respect, preserve and protect all that was provided for we were designated as the steward for these relatives through our use of the sacred gifts of language and thinking.' It is important to recognise the origins of the Rights of Nature movement in Indigenous cultures and wisdom.

These examples of ancient Indigenous worldviews underpin, inform and lead the Rights of Nature movement, as we shall see later, in the examples of Ecuador and Aotearoa/New Zealand.

In addition to Stone and Douglas, people in other parts of the world, such as South America, also played an important role in advocating for the Rights of Nature. Think for example of the Chilean former lawyer Godofredo Stutzin in the 1980s. If we want sustainable and long-term solutions to ecological problems, Stutzin argued, we simply cannot continue to ignore the existence and interests of nature itself. Recognising the Rights of Nature is a first step in putting the entire ecosystem at the centre of the law, rather than just humans.[13] In doing so, we can assume our rightful place as an integral part of the Earth's community.

2

People and ecosystems protected from polluters in Pennsylvania

Tamaqua Borough

More than 34 years after Stone and Douglas' work that laid the foundation for the Rights of Nature, the time had finally come. The Rights of Nature were officially recognised in a piece of legislation, apart from the earlier recognition in the 2002 Diné Fundamental Laws. A tiny borough in the United States state of Pennsylvania made global history in 2006 with their local ordinance appointing ecosystems as 'persons' before the law.

Tamaqua Borough has a little over 7,000 residents and is surrounded by water. Several canals flow right through the downtown area. *Tamaqua* is said to be a Native American name for running water (although others believe it means 'beaver'). Now you might be imagining a picturesque spot where birds whistle and streams babble, but the waterways have been polluted for years due to massive pollution caused by mining in the area. Even the oldest residents cannot remember a time when the river did not run oily yellow on some days due to mining waste. As a result of the pollution, much of the river's biodiversity was lost, and the air was also affected. People fell ill. The impact on residents' health ranged from cancers and infectious diseases to death. For years, residents had to suffer from the pollution. People fell victim to the toxic environment in different parts of rural Pennsylvania. In 1994, 11-year-old Tony Behun died of a bacterial infection after being exposed to the toxic sludge. A year later, 17-year-old Daniel Pennock died of the same contamination.[1]

In the nineteenth and early twentieth centuries, mining was an important industry in the area. When it came to an end, after many years, huge black, gaping pits were left behind in the landscape. The *Environmental Justice Atlas*, an online database on environmental justice, states that some of those pits were twice the size of Tamaqua Borough itself. The owners made these huge pits available to companies to dump a substance consisting of a mixture of river dredge and fly ash, which is released from burning coal. This mixture ended up polluting several streams that flow into a river, affecting a large community that extends beyond Tamaqua: many homes have wells, and river water is the source of the municipal water supply.

One company, Lehigh Coal & Navigation, on learning of the availability of the pits, came up with a proposal. Even though residents had been falling ill from the effects of pollution for years, the company proposed filling the giant wells with mercury-laden fly ash, unmixed with any other substance. Concerns about the air quality in Tamaqua were expressed, but the Pennsylvania Department of Environmental Protection, a government agency charged with protecting land, water, and air, claimed that this would not create hazards for the people and their environment.

The Community Environmental Legal Defense Fund (CELDF), an environmental organisation in the United States that helps people exercise their right to local self-government and advocates for the Rights of Nature, was closely involved with the situation in Tamaqua Borough. They found that the Tamaqua Borough Council officials were claiming not only that dumping fly ash would not be harmful but that Tamaqua residents should be grateful for the opportunities provided by toxic waste being dumped in abandoned mines. The corporation and government agencies, working in tandem, referred to the plan as a 'mine reclamation'. By 'opportunities', they meant revenue: Lehigh Coal & Navigation was to receive permits to dump 700,000 tons of fly ash into the pits and pay $1 per ton to the council. This is one example among many of pure short-term profit being prioritised at the expense of people's health and the wellbeing of nature.

The fact that local politicians focused on the economic benefits of dumping toxic waste and did not consider the long-term effects on humans, animals, and the rest of nature is a recurring problem. All over the world, people opt for short-term solutions without considering the implications for current and future generations. It is a harsh reality: often, the lure of economic profits wins out over protecting the planet.

Power to the people

Residents of Tamaqua had been trying to stand up to the polluters for years, but to no avail. Formally, the companies dumping waste in the pits were in compliance with the laws and regulations governing such activities, but those regulations were not protective, only performative. There came a point when the residents of Tamaqua had had enough.

It was Cathy Miorelli, a high school nurse and member of Tamaqua Borough Council, who contacted CELDF to ask for help.[2] For decades, her community had been a toxic dumping ground for corporations and, as a nurse, she was worried about the effects of these toxins on the community. Her husband, who suffered from a blood condition linked to the toxins, passed away in 2013. He was Miorelli's inspiration for taking a stand, reminding her to keep moving forward, ask questions, and fight for what is right. And so she started to organise the community to stand up against the injustice they were facing.

CELDF's advice to Miorelli and the others was to enact a local law that asserted the right of the community to protect itself from poisoning, but also to recognise and assert the right of local ecosystems to exist and flourish, free from toxic trespass. They decided not to focus only on the politicians, but on the community. If the community recognised that their rights were in danger, and that the ecosystem surrounding them should have a right to exist, thrive, and be restored when damaged, things could potentially change. They proposed their plans in the form of a municipal ordinance, which is a generally binding regulation adopted at the local level, in this case applicable only within Tamaqua Borough. As there was no legal precedent from anywhere else, convincing people to take this approach proved difficult and the chances of it passing were very slim. It was a revolution in the law, as no one had ever tried to do this before.

A local ordinance

After a long and intense campaign of community organising and education, in which residents turned out in large numbers at monthly borough meetings to stand up for their rights, the bill was passed. The ordinance dictates that not only citizens but also natural communities and ecosystems are 'persons' with rights.[3] Every resident has the right to invoke the Rights of Nature. Exactly as Judge Douglas envisioned in 1972: the people who have a meaningful relationship with nature should be able to speak up for it when it is endangered. If nature's right to exist in Tamaqua is threatened, citizens can defend the Rights of Nature in court. According to the ordinance, companies are no longer allowed to act in a way that could endanger the existence and flourishing of natural ecosystems. The law states that dumping toxic substances on land not only endangers human rights but also threatens people's right to life and health, and the existence of nature. This was the first time a piece of legislation recognised that we must respect the existence and flourishing of nature.

The municipal ordinance was passed to protect the health, safety, and welfare of citizens and nature. If the law is violated, a penalty might follow. The fine for a first offence is $750, for the second $1,000, and then $1,000 for each subsequent offence, with each day of non-compliance counting as a separate offence. Eventually, offenders might be sent to prison. So polluters will have to think twice before dumping their toxic waste in Tamaqua.

Passing the ordinance did not come about without controversy. 'State and local politics tried to shut me down, and I was threatened with lawsuits. But I was clear: I'd rather get sued than do nothing while my kids and my community were poisoned. I'd rather get sued than do nothing in the face of so much injustice,' said Miorelli, who started the whole process. A number of council members voted against the law. They were more than happy with the deal in which the council received $1 per ton of fly ash dumped. Some council members even maintained personal relationships with the polluters. They feared they could be sued if nature had its own rights.

The ordinance's opponents also came up with another argument. This new form of legislation would give rights to something that was 'not alive and not a person'. In their view this was impossible. But as we have seen before, it is not a requirement for a person to be human to possess a legal personality. Legal personality is a legal form pursuant to which an entity or organisation can act and perform legal acts. In this way, an organisation's interests can be represented and participate in human society. For example, a legal entity can enter into contracts, file lawsuits, and be sued. As Judge Douglas stated in 1972, if corporations can have legal personality, so should nature. By enabling citizens to act as guardians for nature, the ordinance fosters a sense of community responsibility.

In the case of Tamaqua Borough, Mayor Chris Morrison's vote was the deciding factor in passing the ordinance. 'If I am going to be sued, so be it,' he said. 'You want to take my row house, my little car, good luck, you can have them. We are going to protect our community.'⁴

The ordinance in Tamaqua Borough takes into account that politicians will come and go and that a subsequent council may change policies regarding nature protection. According to the ordinance, citizens are empowered to hold political representatives accountable in the future if they fail to enforce the ban on dumping toxic waste. In doing so, they are not dependent on changing political representatives with different views – this ordinance transcends current political views with the future in mind.

Not everyone was happy with this piece of legislation. The Tamaqua Borough Council claimed that the ordinance was unlawful and not in line with state laws. As far as we know, the ordinance still exists and has never been tested before the courts, because the proposal to dump fly ash in Tamaqua Borough ended up in a figurative pit after the citizens' revolt and the law that followed.

Pittsburgh

The success achieved in Tamaqua Borough was of unprecedented historical importance. The Rights of Nature were no longer just a romantic idea but became a legal reality. The possibility of protecting ecosystems in this way, and establishing a voice for nature in legal systems, did not go unnoticed. In the years following the passing of the ordinance in Tamaqua Borough, dozens of small communities in the United States followed suit through including recognition of the Rights of Nature in (local) laws and regulations.

The same thing happened in Pittsburgh, which, like Tamaqua Borough, is located in the state of Pennsylvania. In 2010, major oil and gas companies expressed an interest in extracting shale gas from the ground beneath this old industrial town. Shale gas – that is, natural gas trapped deep in the ground in shale rock – cannot easily be extracted from the ground. A method called fracking is used for this purpose. This involves injecting a mixture of sand, water, and chemicals into the ground under high pressure, causing cracks in the rock and thereby releasing the gas.

The danger is that the chemicals used for fracking could leak into the ground and contaminate drinking water.[5] In addition, fracturing rock formations more than a mile underground can release radioactive gases that can leak into the soil, pollute groundwater, and affect the atmosphere on the surface. In 2010, Pittsburgh was still recovering from the severe ecological damage caused by industrial activities in previous years. Now there were plans for the next harmful activity in the form of fracking, the long-term effects of which on soil quality and human health were unknown. It came as no surprise that Pittsburgh residents opposed these plans.

Councilman Bill Peduto was also deeply concerned about the plans of the oil and gas companies, who were busy scouting out tracts of land they could use for fracking. A local church had already granted permission to one company to drill for shale gas under its cemetery. In desperation, Peduto emailed everyone he knew, asking: how can Pittsburgh protect its people, environment, and water supply from the negative effects of industrial gas extraction in the city?

This effort seemed to be in vain. Environmental groups, lawyers, and other experts informed Peduto that fracking was permitted under Pennsylvania state laws. There was little a city like Pittsburgh could do about that. After all, in the United States, a city must abide by higher state laws and regulations. The recommendation was: use the current regulations of the city of Pittsburgh to designate areas as so-called *heavy industrial zones*. These zones would be the only areas where fracking was allowed. That way, the damage could be limited to these areas. But Peduto was not satisfied. This solution allowed fracking while he wanted to stop it altogether.[6]

The situation Peduto found himself in is indicative of why current environmental laws do not work: they fail to adequately protect the Earth. They regulate harmful human activity, instead of fully embodying the 'do no harm' principle. There were approximately 38 times as many environmental laws in 2019 as there were in 1972. Yet the United Nations Environment Programme had to admit that all these laws and regulations are *failing* to stop climate change, pollution, and loss of biodiversity and habitats.[7] Things have not changed up to the present day.

We simply cannot solve these kinds of existential environmental problems within the same system that created them in the first place. The moral and legal failures to protect nature run deeper than specific laws and policies – it's a mindset that is embedded in the system itself. The discharge of toxic substances into rivers, for example, is regulated. But the rationale behind such policies is not to protect nature. Emissions must be reduced, but 'only just enough, because the stronger nature gets, the more it can take a beating and social and economic development become possible again' (this is what the Dutch authorities stated about the nitrogen crisis in the Netherlands on a website in 2023).[8] This is indicative of the old Western worldview in which nature serves humans. Environmental regulations are still based on the extent to which we can 'allow' dangerous or harmful plans. This was also the case in Pittsburgh. Under existing law, even though damage by fracking could be mitigated, it would still be allowed to happen.

A new approach

Fortunately, the CELDF – the same environmental organisation that helped realise the Rights of Nature in Tamaqua Borough – came up with a solution. From its previous experiences, the organisation had learned to look for new approaches to protect nature, rather than working through the outdated legal system. The organisations that had previously worked with council member Peduto to find solutions to the threat of fracking only came up with recommendations that fell within that framework.

Now, instead of investigating what was possible within current laws and regulations, the CELDF came up with the idea of a new law. A law that would protect both the rights of citizens and natural ecosystems and communities. Citizens would have the right to clean air and pure water, and nature would have the right to exist, flourish and be free of pollution. Then citizens, with the law as their weapon, could effectively challenge the fracking plans.

Peduto approved of the plan. He pleaded the case to his council group of experts: a new law might seem like a controversial approach, but it seemed to be the only option to stop fracking in the city. After citizens showed mass support for the movement to protect human rights as well as nature, even those opposed to this in Pittsburgh council had no other choice than to get to work on the Rights of Nature.

The law took the form of a city ordinance. It resembled the ordinance passed in Tamaqua Borough, but in this case applied only to the city of Pittsburgh. The city's oil and gas industry threatened legal action to overturn the ordinance. They felt cornered. But their threats were in vain. The ordinance was passed unanimously by local council members. And that was because citizens had a say in city council meetings and showed massive support for this new approach. Thus, in November 2010, Pittsburgh made history by becoming the first major American city to recognise the Rights of Nature.

Under the law, all residents, natural communities, and eco-systems in Pittsburgh have a fundamental and inalienable right to sustainably access, use, consume, and preserve water drawn from natural water cycles that sustain life in the city.[9] In addition, natural communities and ecosystems, including but not limited to wetlands, streams, rivers, and other water systems, have the fundamental right to exist and flourish in Pittsburgh. The rights of citizens and nature are protected, thanks to the law, by prohibiting future industrial gas extraction in the city.

Pittsburgh residents watch over the Rights of Nature in their city. They have been empowered to enforce these rights and can appear in court on behalf of nature, as is the case in Tamaqua Borough. Citizens can stand up to polluters by invoking this law, not only on their own behalf, but also on behalf of nature.

Local justice

Since the passing of the law in Pittsburgh, no new fracking has taken place within the city limits, says education director Ben Price of CELDF. The pending contract that the local church was considering for fracking under the cemetery became void. Only the projects that had already begun in the city before the ordinance was passed were allowed to continue, and they did not include fracking.[10]

This was a victory for Pittsburgh residents and future generations. Well, just for city residents, maybe. It seems that fracking activities are now moving to the suburbs. Years after the passing of the ordinance, there were plans to build two fracking wells within a mile and a half of an elementary school in a poor, vulnerable community.[11] This community is referred to as an 'environmental justice community'. According to Pennsylvania, these are places where at least 20 per cent of the population lives at or below the federal poverty line and at least 30 per cent have identified as non-white. These types of communities often face extreme poverty, racism, and pollution.

What we see happening here is a local example of a global justice problem. Daphina Misiedjan, associate professor of human rights and environment at the International Institute of Social Studies, concludes that large vulnerable communities usually lose out in environmental or climate cases as powerful small groups determine the lives of such communities. In 2023, the Pennsylvania Department of Health researched the impacts of fracking and results showed increased risk of childhood cancer, asthma, and low birth weights for people living near fracking wells. And yet the residents are left to their own devices and fracking continues.[12]

While local legislation may provide protection within the boundaries of towns, they have the potential to shift the problems to poor communities. There needs to be room for both environmental and social justice, Misiedjan argues. In the next chapter, on Florida, we will see that state laws can undermine the local recognition of the Rights of Nature by virtue of being hierarchically higher in rank.

It is, therefore, questionable whether local laws are the most effective way of recognising the Rights of Nature. However, what such laws do illustrate is that they can make a real difference at a local level. People and ecosystems are now protected from polluters in Tamaqua Borough and Pittsburgh. It is no coincidence that more and more communities across the United States are following suit with similar initiatives for the Rights of Nature.

3

Water bodies appear before judges in Florida

Citizens standing up for the rights of water

Florida is a place where water breathes life into the landscape: from swampy marshes, secret waterfalls to mangrove forests. At its heart lie the Everglades: a vast marsh landscape with rivers, creeks, and forests, providing an important source of freshwater. Here, majestic cranes soar, alligators glide through the waters, and elusive Florida panthers and black bears roam the pathways. This natural sanctuary, celebrated worldwide as a national park and recognised as a World Heritage site, embodies Florida's beauty and biodiversity; it is a place to be protected and cherished.

And yet those unique ecosystems and wildlife in Florida are under serious threat. In recent decades, Florida has forfeited large supplies of freshwater by draining marshes for construction projects, but also for agricultural irrigation. A water crisis is looming by 2030, when it is estimated that Florida's demand for fresh water will have increased by 28 per cent compared to 2005.[1] According to the Florida Rights of Nature Network:

Over the past 50 years, red tides in Florida have grown dramatically in frequency and duration. Between 1878 and

1994, there were 64 months of red tide. In the following 24 years, there were 184. Florida has issued 23,000 pollution permits to industries, 2,440 of the 4,393 of its waterways have been declared impaired, 50,000 tons of phosphorus sit at the bottom of Lake Okeechobee, and 'mismanagement of natural resources has turned one of the building blocks of life [blue-green algae] into a potential monster.' Our regulatory system, highly subject to corporate influence and changing political winds, has failed us and the ecosystems upon which we depend.[2]

Overconsumption, pollution, and the effects of climate change are threatening the future of freshwater and aquifers in Florida. Florida's waters are suffering because, until recently, they had no voice or ability to stand up for their interests. Environmental organisations had been sounding the alarm over the water crisis for decades, but to no avail.

It is time to hear the voices of the waters in Florida, according to Chuck O'Neal, a local citizen and president of the Florida Rights of Nature Network. Chuck has a lifelong attachment to Florida's natural beauty and is an award-winning conservation advocate. Together with concerned citizens and the Center for Democratic and Environmental Rights (CDER), an organisation working with governments, tribal nations, Indigenous communities, civil society, and grassroots activists to advance democratic and environmental rights, he advocated for the recognition of the rights of waters in Orange County. A legislative measure was proposed for the Orange County charter – a local constitution that applies only in Orange County. This charter said nothing about the Rights of Nature.

After an intensive lobbying process, O'Neal and his colleagues succeeded: in November 2020, a vote for the Rights of Nature amendment to be added to the charter passed with a majority of 89 per cent.[3] According to this amendment, the Wekiva River, the Econlockhatchee River, and all other waterways within the boundaries of Orange County have rights. They have the right to exist, to flow, to be protected from pollution, and the right to maintain a healthy ecosystem. Not only do the waterways have rights: Orange County residents also have a right to clean water.

In Orange County, all citizens, municipalities, and government agencies have *legal standing*, and thus the power to enforce water rights in court. To do so, they may advocate on behalf of the waterways. To *Reasons to be Cheerful*, O'Neal said:

> The amendment grants nature four rights: the right to exist, to flow, to be protected against pollution and to maintain a healthy ecosystem. That, paired with the human right for all citizens to have clean water, went on the ballot and passed in 2020 with 89 per cent of the votes. I consider this monumental for a county of 1.4 million people.[4]

Orange County became the largest municipality in the United States to date where the Rights of Nature have been recognised by law. Thomas Linzey, senior legal counsel at the CDER, stated that they were 'looking forward to assisting the people of Orange County to enforce and defend this measure, and to helping people across Florida to adopt similar measures to protect Florida's threatened rivers, streams, bays, and watersheds'.

Higher political powers

While Orange County was celebrating this historical move, the state of Florida was feeling the heat. A few months before voting on the Orange County legislative amendment took place, the Florida Legislature included a clause against the Rights of Nature in Senate Bill 712 in June 2020.[5] This bill is of higher authority than laws or regulations enacted at the county level, and the authority of local counties to enforce the Rights of Nature and human rights to the laws of the state of Florida is subordinate to this bill.

Practically, that means the State of Florida does not recognise the Rights of Nature of local governments, such as Orange County. Be it through a regulation, ordinance, rule, or any other form of law or rule, local governments in Florida cannot recognise or grant certain legal rights to plants, animals, waterways, or other parts of the natural environment that are not a person or political subdivision. Given the timing of the bill, it appears that it was passed to counteract the Rights of Nature amendment that had been added to the Orange County charter.[6]

Concerned citizens argue that this bill was passed because the state of Florida fears the effects of the Rights of Nature, according to which citizens could directly stand up to government policies. Karl Deigert, initiator of Rights of Nature in Lee County, said,

Municipal and corporate economic actors recognise Rights of Nature laws as so highly effective as to regard them as heresy to their exploitative activities against nature; hence, they moved Florida legislators to draft language stripping a community's right to create new laws protecting the health, safety and welfare of the citizenry.[7]

An uphill battle

Back to the Rights of Nature amendment in Orange County. In April 2021, less than six months after the charter was amended, O'Neal filed a lawsuit on behalf of the Wild Cypress and Boggy streams, Crosby Island wetlands and Hart and Mary Jane lakes.[8] This was a lawsuit against the developer Beachline South Residential, LLC, which had plans to fill 1,900 acres of the area with homes and offices. In the same case, the Florida Department of Environmental Protection, the state agency responsible for issuing permits for Beachline's project, was also tried.

Using 1,900 acres for housing development is no small matter. The proposed project would destroy and pollute an area the size of 1,075 soccer fields. One of the arguments of the lawyer representing the water bodies was that the natural flow of water to the many lakes would be restricted by the housing development. Local ecosystems would be destroyed, thus threatening the waters' very existence. Storage systems needed to be built for excess water, for which vast areas of wetlands would need to be sacrificed. It was the first case of its kind in the United States: never before had a marsh, two streams and two lakes appeared in court to argue for their own rights, represented by a human being. According to O'Neal:

This lawsuit poses the question of whether the interests of one development corporation should outweigh the interests of over half a million Orange County voters and the existence of streams, marshes, lakes, and wetlands important to the region. The plaintiff-waterways represented in this action deserve more than just their day in court – they need to have even their most basic right to exist protected. For too long our legislators have told the public we need balance between commerce and Nature and then folded to pressure from commerce to permit egregious exploitation.

A development permit from the city of Orlando and a dredging and fill permit from the Florida Department of Environmental Protection were required for the construction of the excess water storage facility. O'Neal tried to use the lawsuit to prevent these permits from being granted. The developer and the Florida government argued that the court case could not move forward. According to the Florida state bill, local governmental laws and regulations concerning the Rights of Nature are not recognised by the courts. Thus, the attested rights for waters in Orange County on a local level would be invalid. Moreover, the developer and the government claimed that the court where the case had been heard was not the correct forum given that the case was about permits. According to them, this was an administrative matter that should be dealt with by a different, administrative court.

Much to O'Neal's disappointment, the first judge, who considered the case in July 2022, ruled that the Rights of Nature in Orange County were indeed not in line with the state bill. State law had a higher authority and applied in this case. The waters in Orange County could have no rights, the judge ruled. O'Neal's group, Speak Up Wekiva, Inc., appealed, but in January 2024, the 6th District Court of Appeal upheld the decision.

O'Neal continues to seek new legal avenues to stand up for the water bodies in Orange County. 'It's certainly an uphill battle in this state,' he explains. 'We have to keep in mind that we are at the forefront of a legal concept that will someday be accepted as commonplace: "Well, of course nature has rights." But the lumps go to those first through the door, or wall, as it may be.' This battle is proving difficult, because of the influence of economic factors on politics, and conflicts with state and federal regulations.

The Florida Right to Clean Water Initiative

The recognition of the Rights of Nature is also being advocated for at the state level in Florida. For example, the Right to Clean Water Initiative advocates for the right to clean water for all residents and waters in Florida. Waters should have the right to exist, flow, be protected from pollution, and maintain a healthy ecosystem. Realising those rights requires local legislation. Those rights were recognised in Orange County, although we will now need to wait and see what happens to the amendment in light of the ruling in the case described in the previous section. However, it is not only important that the Rights of Nature are enshrined in law, but that they are properly enforced and implemented.

The latter remains a difficult principle for the Rights of Nature movement. A river or stream is unable to indicate in human language when its rights are being violated or when preventive action is required. Therefore, any citizen, non-profit organisation, or government agency should be authorised to stand up for the rights of water bodies, according to the initiative.

With the Right to Clean Water Initiative, citizens sought to enshrine the rights of waterways and citizens in the Florida Constitution,[9] which is the supreme law within the state of Florida, and was due to be revised in 2022. More than 900,000 supporting signatures were needed for the proposed amendment to be added to the Florida Constitution.[10] Due in part to the Covid-19 pandemic and the fact that the Right to Clean Water Initiative's campaign therefore ran over a shorter time than had been planned, the minimum number of signatures required to support the amendment was not met.

Besides the impact of the Covid-19 pandemic, the initiative was not welcomed by everyone in conservative Florida. During the campaign, lawyer and columnist Wesley J. Smith urged people not to sign the initiative. Granting rights to water was a terrible policy, he said: its intended and unintended consequences could even be called anti-human. If a swamp had the right to exist, it could lead to a ban on draining that area. Building projects could be stopped.[11]

Smith was, in fact, spot on with his column. Instead of just considering the interests of developers and government agencies, the initiative for the rights of water forces people to consider the interests of water bodies rather than solely human concerns.

Despite setbacks, the Right to Clean Water Initiative continues its work, albeit with a different focus. The people involved are now working on getting the human right of citizens to clean water recognised, because they believe that a Rights of Nature law at the state level will not receive sufficient support in the current political climate. Important political players in Florida will most likely oppose such a law. The Right to Clean Water Initiative attempted to add a constitutional amendment ensuring a fundamental right to clean water to the 2024 ballot but, by late 2023, they had collected only about 115,000 of the 900,000 signatures required. As a result, the advocates shifted their target to the 2026 ballot and began their initiative anew in March 2024. The recognition of this right would also enable citizens to sue state agencies for actions that threaten or harm Florida's water bodies.

The future of waters in Florida

The court cases involving the water bodies in Orange County and the Right to Clean Water Initiative demonstrate that it is difficult to establish the Rights of Nature when there are higher political powers working against it. The judge in the Orange County lawsuit had a unique opportunity to determine the ways in which the water bodies' right to exist would need to be respected in projects. A construction project that would require clearing an area the size of 1,075 soccer fields runs counter to the rights of Orange County's water bodies. Earlier, in 2021, Mari Margil, the executive director at CDER, said:

> Around the world and across the United States, a new system of environmental protection is emerging – one that recognises waterways and other ecosystems as having legally enforceable rights. This new system is a response to the current regulatory system that serves to permit ongoing harms to the natural environment. Florida is the epicentre of this shift toward waterway rights for good reason, because the state government continues to approve of the destruction of wetlands and other waterways. It is long past

time to recognise that we are dependent on nature, and the continued destruction of nature needs to stop.[12]

The fact that the judge had to dismiss the case because of a higher and conflicting Florida state law shows that local laws – at least in the United States – are fragile. They are subordinate to the higher laws of the state, and therefore to higher-level political powers. In the case of Orange County, 89 per cent of voters voted in favour of the amendment for the rights of waterways. The people had spoken in favour of the Rights of Nature, but the amendment to the charter was quashed at a higher level. It seems it is still up to concerned (local) citizens like O'Neal to keep on pressing and advocating for the recognition and enforcement of the Rights of Nature.

4

A river with legal personality in Aotearoa/New Zealand

'I am the river, the river is me'

Aotearoa/New Zealand may not be the first country that comes to mind when thinking about groundbreaking change, but it has long been a pioneer in progressive legal reforms. In 1893, it became the first country in the world to grant women the right to vote. In 1999, it amended its Animal Welfare Act to include protections for non-human primates such as gorillas, chimpanzees, and orangutans, with an explicit focus on their individual interests. Nowadays, Aotearoa/New Zealand is known as a pioneer in the Rights of Nature. It has assigned legal personality to the Te Urewera (a former national park), the Whanganui River, and Mount Taranaki.

The Rights of Nature in Aotearoa/New Zealand have everything to do with the Māori, the first inhabitants of Aotearoa (the Māori name for the land known by most as New Zealand). The recognition of the Rights of Nature was preceded by a long, painful history that began with the arrival of British settlers. In 1840, the British and the Māori signed the Treaty of Waitangi, also known as *Te Tiriti o Waitangi*, which became Aotearoa/New Zealand's founding document and guided the relationship between the British Crown and the Māori. The treaty agreed on the division of land. The

Māori wanted to preserve their centuries-old traditions, and the treaty gave them the right to exclusive and undisturbed possession of their own land, forests, and fisheries.

The treaty was drafted in both English and Māori, which led to different interpretations and debates on its wording and intention.[1] Provisions relating to property were difficult to translate into Māori. The Māori do not work with the concept of ownership (of land) as people in the West understand the concept. Consequently, the treaty was interpreted differently by both parties. After the Māori had lived in harmony with nature for generations, nature was now subjugated, exploited, and destroyed by the Crown (the constitutional office of Aotearoa/New Zealand). It was the beginning of years of conflict and a struggle by the Māori to address this colonial injustice. The intention of the treaty was to establish an equal partnership, but this proved not to be adhered to in practice.

Part of the conflict concerned the mystical Whanganui River, the third longest river in the North Island of Aotearoa/New Zealand. According to the Māori, the river is *Te Awa Tupua*: a living and indivisible whole, from its source in the mountains to where it joins the sea. The Whanganui is a wild river, surrounded by dense forest and towering rocks – a place that cannot be owned by humans.

The people of the Whanganui Māori called the Ngāti Hau, including the *iwi* (groups) and *hapū* (sub-groups) of the Whanganui River, have lived alongside the river for centuries and depend on it for food, drink, medicine, and ceremonies. The river not only feeds them in their basic needs. Spiritually, they regard the river as a spiritual ancestor. An expressive statement about their relationship to the Whanganui River is '*Ko au te Awa, ko te Awa ko au*' – 'I am the river, the river is me.'

With the arrival of the British settlers, the management of the river changed. Instead of the river being seen as an indivisible whole, it was divided into manageable portions with boundaries. Nature became property and different people owned pieces of land bordering the river. Instead of living in harmony with the river, as the peoples of the Whanganui River had done for centuries, the Crown had other plans for it. They removed gravel from the river to build railroads. They allowed businesses to discharge waste into the river; they built dams to control how the river flowed and limited its natural rapids so boats could navigate it more easily. All these interventions caused the condition of the river to deteriorate and prevented the peoples of the Whanganui River from using it as they had done before. A legal battle spanning more than 150 years ensued, during which the tribes tried to address this injustice.

In the 1970s, the Crown initiated a process aimed at repairing the damage done to the Māori and the land. The Waitangi Tribunal was established to investigate historical violations of the treaty and make recommendations for their redress. In 1999, a Whanganui River enquiry came before the Waitangi Tribunal. The tribunal recommended returning the river's property rights to the peoples of the Whanganui River, after which a nearly 20-year negotiation period began. But the Crown maintained that the river could not be owned by the peoples of the Whanganui River, since under Aotearoa/New Zealand common law it is assumed no one can 'own' water.

A compromise was reached in 2017: the river would have its own legal personality. When a journalist from the CNN asked Gerrard Albert, one of the Māori leaders for the Whanganui River, if he had heard of Professor Stone, he replied: 'I didn't have a clue who he was.' His fight was the one his forefathers had started decades ago, over legal recognition of Māori rights. By winning recognition through the compromise over the Whanganui River, the suffering of his elders had not been in vain and the rights of future generations of Māori were now recognised through this law.

What is more absurd?

In 2017, the Te Awa Tupua Act was passed which made the Whanganui River a legal person.[2] The act considers the Whanganui River and its tributaries, from the mountains to the sea, as an indivisible and living whole, including physical and metaphysical elements. The Whanganui is considered a spiritual and physical entity that sustains life in the river as well as the tribes. The act reads like poetry through its use of Māori words and sayings about the river. It recognises that the peoples of the Whanganui River have an inalienable connection to the river and bear responsibility for its health and wellbeing. The river consists of aquatic flora and fauna, floodplain forests, tributaries, groundwater, rocks, soil, and banks. The law even specifies that 'the airspace above the water' is included in the definition of the bed of the Whanganui River. All of these must be protected because the health of all these natural elements affects the wellbeing of the river's ecosystem. This shows that this act understands how all elements of the river are interconnected and dependent on its wellbeing.

This is a major change from the previous policy regarding the river. Rather than treating the river as a patchwork with separated parts, the river has now become one indivisible whole, to be legally treated as such. Chris Finlayson, the

Aotearoa/New Zealand minister responsible for negotiations at the time, said:

> None of this was particularly radical or groundbreaking. In fact, the European centric way of thinking about land was 'weird'. What is more absurd? To look at a river as a single holistic entity from where it's formed out to the sea, to saying we're going to divide the river up? That's a pretty potty way of thinking about things in my view.[3]

This was not the first time Aotearoa/New Zealand recognised the Rights of Nature: in 2014, a former national park, the Te Urewera territory, was granted legal personality and in 2024, Mount Taranaki officially became a legal person as well.

The Whanganui River is thus a legal person and has all the consequent rights, powers, duties, and liabilities. In practice, these are mediated by the representatives, and have not been used in the same way as they are for corporations. It is often said that legal personhood makes the Whanganui River own itself. In fact, this is not entirely correct. In practice, existing property rights of private persons are not affected by this law. The farmer who owns a plot of land along the river can keep it. Businesses along the river, including a hydroelectric plant, also retain property rights. But the Crown parts of the bed of the river have been transferred to the river as a legal entity and can no longer be sold or transferred. A non-ownership model means that the river is not owned by any entity, but is a legal person with rights and interests that are protected by its guardians.

As a legal person, the Whanganui River can be held liable for damages in its capacity of owner, for example, if the river causes damage to someone else's property.[4] We might wonder: would it be possible – if the river were to flood in the future, for example due to the effects of climate change – that a farmer with land bordering the river could claim compensation? At the same time, these are questions that are solely asked by Western scholars. Elizabeth Macpherson, a professor specialising in environmental law and Indigenous peoples in Aotearoa/New Zealand, reaffirmed that most of the scholarly engagement with the Whanganui legal model comes from outside Aotearoa/New Zealand, though its implications reach far beyond legal innovation.

A part of the legal framework for the representation of the river is the *Te Pou Tupua*, humans acting as the 'human face' and in the name of the Whanganui River. *Te Pou Tupua* consists of two to six representatives of the Crown and representatives of the peoples of the Whanganui river. Both parties can choose who they appoint to this position. They must promote and protect the health of the river. *Te Pou Tupua* can act on behalf of and in the best interests of the river, just like the representatives of a company.

An advisory group known as *Te Karewao* was established to provide advice and support to *Te Pou Tupua* in carrying out its mandate. The *Te Kōpuka* strategy group also supports the representatives on matters of strategy, to monitor, review, and provide a forum for discussions on issues relating to the health and wellbeing of the river.

Regarding the selection of these representatives, one might ask: can someone from the same government that previously oversaw the degradation of the river now serve as one of its representatives? Wouldn't that be a conflict of interest? The law in fact is designed to set up a robust legal structure that limits the representatives' mandate. They can only represent the interests of the river and are the 'human face' of the river. Their duties are clear. They cannot represent interests other than those of the river. There are mechanisms in place to manage conflicts and maintain the river's wellbeing as the primary focus.

The whole question of who gets to represent nature is one of particular difficulty. In the chapter on Spain, we will see that guardianship for nature can also be arranged differently, with the participation of citizens and scientists. Representation is an important challenge within the Rights of Nature movement: who can best represent nature and its interests? The clear structure of checks and balances for the Whanganui River is a great example for the rest of the world in addressing the difficulties around appointing representatives for nature.

Dialogue over legal action

The government provided NZ $1 million for the effectuation of the settlement of all the treaty's claims concerning the river. Gerrard Albert, the Māori leader during the Whanganui negotiations, considers the river's governance model a success. He told British newspaper the *Guardian*, 'We fought to find an approximation in law so that all others can understand that from our perspective treating the river as a living entity is the correct way to approach it: as an indivisible whole, instead of the traditional model for the last hundred years of treating it from a perspective of ownership and management.'[5]

The current model significantly changes the way the local people are included in decisions concerning the river. The legal personhood of the Whanganui River was never about bringing legal cases. The law on the river's legal personhood is an outcome of a negotiated settlement of a long-running conflict over the river's ownership and governance between the government and the Māori. It was about restoring justice – and legal personhood was part of a broader model of collaborative governance and a compromise between the demands of the government and the Māori. Erin O'Donnell, water law expert at the University of Melbourne, told CNN: 'When we see rivers as living beings that are part of our community then that does actually profoundly change the way we speak about them, the way we make laws about them, the way we make decisions about them.'[6]

Aotearoa/New Zealand is often cited as the prime example of Rights of Nature, but as an acquaintance of Minister Finlayson once noted, the Rights of Nature in Aotearoa/New Zealand are: 'internationally hot, domestically not'.[7] Nevertheless, Finlayson says Aotearoa/New Zealand can be an example of how two worldviews – Western and Māori – can be united in law. Since the recognition of Whanganui's legal personality, there has been a slow but steady shift. Along its banks, projects are being set up to restore the river and more attention is being paid to the role of the Māori in this process. Such a paradigm shift may take generations, but enshrining a different relationship to nature in law is an important first step. It may take decades for people to shred the worldview that humans are masters over the river, but the first step towards a harmonious relationship with the river has been taken.

The human face of the river

The Aotearoa/New Zealand Act ensures that the Whanganui River now has human faces representing its interests, and that its voice must be heard in any development that may affect the river. Since 2017, there have been no lawsuits concerning the river's legal personality. River representatives are involved at an early stage in decisions that may affect the natural environment. This legal status encourages dialogue, eliminating the need for litigation.

In the past, there were plans for a bicycle bridge to be built across the river. As the representatives of the Whanganui were not consulted, it was suggested this could lead to conflict. Ultimately, the situation was resolved by consulting the representatives, and the bridge was built, without any lawsuits.[8] When people asked Māori leader Albert if he would sue polluters now that the river has legal personality, he responded, somewhat surprisingly: 'When you've spent 150 years yourself of being thrown around and abused, why would we seek to be punitive and do the same thing to others? [Legal personhood] is a paradigm shift, first and foremost.'

To date, the Whanganui's legal personality has been a success but, at the same time, it does raise major questions about the river's duties and liabilities. According to the act, the Whanganui has all the attendant rights, powers, duties, and liabilities of a legal person. It is, therefore, not weird to ask: is legal personality for nature really the best way of protecting its rights, if by doing so we become entangled in a legal web with complicated obstacles? This would seem to suggest that we may remain stuck in the old system, when what we really want is to work towards a new way of coexisting with the rest of nature.

We can establish the Rights of Nature in other ways apart from assigning legal personality, as later examples in this book will illustrate. Still, Aotearoa/New Zealand shows that it can be done and that it works. The legal personality of the Whanganui River illustrates that the Rights of Nature is about dialogue and the inclusion of interests of nature and local people, not just about litigation.

5

A difficult struggle for sacred rivers in India

A sacred status

In 1997, Space Shuttle Columbia took a series of photographs of the Earth during mission STS-87, on which the 2,510-kilometre-long Ganga River was clearly visible. With its thousands of winding tributaries and forks, the river looks as if it has thousands of blood vessels.[1] The Ganga River, better known in Europe as the Ganges, emerges from the Bhagirathi River that rises from the Gangotri glacier in the Himalayan mountains in India, passes through Bangladesh and flows into the Bay of Bengal.

For centuries, the river has been considered sacred by Hindus and worshipped in the form of the river goddess Ganga.[2] Ganga is often depicted in Indian art as a beautiful woman riding the Makara. The Makara is a divine creature that resembles a crocodile with the tail of a fish. The goddess often holds an overflowing jug in her hands, indicating the abundance and fertility of nature. Bathing in the Ganga River allows you to wash away your sins. The ashes and bodies of deceased Hindus are often cast into the river to promote a peaceful farewell from this earth. Living persons depend on the river for their livelihood in addition to having a spiritual relationship with it: over 4 million people live near the river and use its water for cooking, washing and as drinking water.[3] This is why the river is also called *Ganga Maa*, Mother Ganga. It nourishes and nurtures, brings life, and attracts life.

One of the largest tributaries of the Ganga River is the Yamuna. This river rises from the glacier Yamuntori in the Indian state of Uttarakhand and flows to the south, where it merges with the Ganga River. This river is also considered sacred by Hindus and worshipped in the form of a river goddess: Yamuna. Yamuna is often depicted as a beautiful girl on the banks of the river, standing on a turtle while holding a water pot. You can bathe in the Yamuna River to absolve yourself of your sins. Beautiful temples lining the riverbanks are dedicated to Yamuna.

It is somewhat ironic that, despite their sacred status, the Ganga and Yamuna rivers are among the most polluted in the world. Inadequate or non-existent sewage and rubbish systems lead to the human and other waste from over 4 million local households ending up in their waters. Waste from slaughterhouses, hospitals, and textile factories is dumped in these rivers. Even the sacred status of these rivers leads to pollution: millions of people make offerings for the rivers in the form of chemically treated flowers and plastics that pollute the water.

Rivers are not only threatened by pollution. Dams alter the natural flow of rivers, and the rainy season is unpredictable due to the effects of climate change. The glaciers in the mountains that feed the rivers are melting away and the rivers are running dry. This is a major threat to the people who depend on the rivers for their livelihood. Likewise, endangered species such as the Ganges dolphin and the Asian elephant that live along the banks of the Yamuna River are dependent on the wellbeing of the river.

The government has recognised the pollution of these rivers as a problem for years, but little is being done about it. Complexities relating to population density and illegal activities along the riverbanks has led to governments failing to address the pollution. Promises to restore the rivers have been made repeatedly but are not followed up with action.

Judges speaking out

The movement for the recognition of the Rights of Nature is thriving in several places in India. In 2013, an initiative calling for the recognition of the rights of the Ganga River – the National Ganga Rights Movement – was formed. The movement argued that the river should have the right to exist and flourish. It should be protected from pollution and therefore the government, civil society and citizens of India should be able to take action on behalf of the river when its rights are threatened.

Action is urgently needed, right now. The river is being polluted by nearly 3 billion gallons of sewage and chemical waste on a day-to-day basis. That is why a National Ganga River Rights Act was drafted in 2016, a bill that seeks to establish the rights of the Ganga River and its watershed, so that they can be protected. The National Ganga River Rights Act 'specifically designates remedies through a rights-based framework so that our National River, and the 500 million people and countless species of plants and wildlife that depend on it, may be enabled to survive and thrive'.[4] The Act also seeks to establish the power of citizens to enforce and defend the rights of the Ganga River. Little information is available about the current status of the Act. We do know that the bill has not yet been passed into law.

*   *   *

A lawsuit concerning the Ganga and Yamuna rivers marked a step forward for the Rights of Nature in India. It began in 2014, when Mohammad Salim, who lives in the state of Uttarakhand, became concerned about illegal structures being built along the Ganga River and the overall degradation of the river. He filed a petition with the High Court of Uttarakhand.[5] In petition proceedings, unlike writ proceedings, you can petition a judge directly for a ruling.

In his request, Salim pleaded for action by the governments of Uttar Pradesh and Uttarakhand, two states in northern India through which the Ganga River flows. These states were doing nothing to stop pollution of the river, Salim argued. The Yamuna became involved in the case because Salim advocated for a better connection of the ownership and governance of both rivers, currently divided between the state governments of Attarakhand and Uttar Pradesh. He said the division of ownership of the rivers was proving to be ineffective.

In December 2016, the court ordered the local governments along the Ganga River to remove all (illegal) parties from the land, to install a board of directors for the Ganga within three months, and to ban mining in the river floodplain.[6] Several months later, the matter came before the same court again. No real action had been taken. The judges expressed their displeasure. Because local governments were failing to protect the rivers, they argued, the Ganga and Yamuna were losing the very essence of their existence. The rivers were suffering because of pollution and because of this exceptional situation, exceptional measures were called for.

The second time this case came before the courts, the judges made an extraordinary ruling. It was now March 2017, shortly after the Whanganui River in Aotearoa/New Zealand had been recognised as a legal person. The Indian judges argued that the Ganga and Yamuna should also be legal persons and should be treated as *living* beings. They are not just bodies of water, they argued, because it is scientifically proven that rivers are alive. A legal status belongs not only to the rivers themselves, but also to the glaciers that 'feed' them, and to the tributaries and all streams connected to them.

This had never been argued before in India. The legal personality argument was based on an earlier ruling on Hindu idols (the physical manifestations of Hindu gods). According to the Supreme Court of India, idols could have legal personality. Human representatives were appointed to act in the interest of the idols.

The court in Uttarakhand was building on that argument in the ruling on legal personality for the rivers Ganga and the Yamuna. The Indian Water Resources Minister, Uma Bharti, said afterwards: 'We have always considered Ganga as a mother and a mother is a living person. The court has endorsed our point of view.'[7]

On the issue of river representation, the court cited the concept of *parens patriae*, meaning 'parent of the nation' in Latin. This is a public order power of the state through which protection can be secured for any individual, child, or animal in need of protection. Three people were appointed as guardians of the river: the director of the Namami Gange Programme, which was set up by local governments in 2015 to restore and preserve the Ganga, and the chief secretary and the attorney general of Uttarakhand. They were mandated to protect the rivers' legal status and promote their health and wellbeing.

Practical implications

The groundbreaking ruling on the legal personality of the rivers did not hold up. The Uttarakhand authorities challenged the decision before the Supreme Court of India (which is a higher court than the High Court of Uttarakhand), arguing that legal personality for rivers was legally untenable. Legal personality for rivers, they said, raises a lot of practical issues. How do we deal with rivers that also flow through other countries? The Ganga River also flows through Bangladesh.

Those fighting the ruling questioned whether the guardians could be held liable if the rivers were to cause floods and cause damage to landowners. Local communities are directly dependent on the rivers for their livelihood. If small farmers draw water from them for irrigation, can they be sued for violating the rivers' rights? The Supreme Court agreed with this line of argument and overturned the earlier ruling by the judges in Uttarakhand on the legal personality of the rivers because of the ambiguities surrounding this status.

It is understandable that the Supreme Court found the Uttarakhand judges' ruling on legal personality for the rivers to be unclear. Unlike the legal personality for the Whanganui River in Aotearoa/New Zealand, a legal construction that has a clear mandate, the ruling on legal personality for the Ganga and Yamuna was vague. The judges in Uttarakhand ruled that the rivers were legal persons, but said nothing about the practical implications of this: how were challenges faced by the rivers, such as illegal discharges, to be handled? Nor had the local communities surrounding the rivers, from farmers to fishermen, been involved in the ruling. Those people had not been given the opportunity to speak on behalf of the river – even though they depended on it for their livelihood. A new form of policy concerning the river would certainly affect their daily lives, perhaps in a positive way, and yet they were largely ignored during this process.

It was, all in all, a missed opportunity. There are issues that need deeper understanding surrounding legal personality for rivers, but the concept can be implemented, and it can be effective. The example of Aotearoa/New Zealand illustrates that. A few years later, the concept of rights for rivers would prove viable, not only in faraway countries, but also in the land of India's neighbour Bangladesh.

Bangladesh

The story of river rights in Bangladesh began in 2016, when *The Daily Star* published an article on the state of the Turag River with an alarming headline: 'It's time to declare the Turag River dead'.[8] The river is so heavily polluted and degraded that we should consider it dead, the newspaper wrote. The article triggered public outrage. An investigation into pollution of the Turag River had been ongoing for some time, but the non-profit organisation Human Rights and Peace for Bangladesh decided that the time for action had now come. They petitioned the High Court Division of the Bangladesh Supreme Court shortly after the article appeared in *The Daily Star*.

The petition claimed the government should be held liable for the structures and activities along the river that had caused the river to be degraded and polluted. Inspired by a public conference during which rights for rivers were discussed, the court declared the Turag River a legal entity in 2019.[9] This legal status applied to over 200 rivers in the country, the judges said, and was accompanied by 17 concrete action points aimed at restoring and protecting the rivers of Bangladesh. Mohammad Abdul Matin, secretary of the environmental group Bangladesh Poribesh Andolon, told NPR: 'The river is now considered by law, by code, a living entity, so you'll have to face the consequence by law if you do anything that kills the river.'[10]

One of the action points related to the representation of the rivers, for which a special commission was to be appointed. That commission is required to protect and conserve the rivers. All relevant authorities wanting to set up new projects around rivers in Bangladesh now had to discuss them with the special commission first. The commission acts as the guardian defending the rights of the rivers.

The legal group Anima Mundi Law Initiative reported in 2021 that the ruling on rights for the rivers of Bangladesh had brought some results, for example, along the banks of rivers in the capital Dhaka, more than four thousand illegal settlements had been cleared and parcels of land restored.[11] Many challenges remain. But it is interesting to explore why legal personality for rivers was considered possible in Bangladesh, it was considered legally unfeasible in India.

Research in collaboration with the local community

Since 2020, Indian activist and researcher Shrishtee Bajpai has been engaging in dialogue with experts and residents along the rivers in India to explore what legal personality might mean for the rivers. One of the problems with the judicial ruling on the Ganga and Yamuna rivers, according to Bajpai, was that it was not *bottom-up*, it did not involve and engage local communities.

The implications of acknowledging nature as a legal person are immense. A different democratic system, in which guardians are appointed to speak on behalf of nature, needs to be established. This must be done in consultation with the people who depend on the river for their livelihood. According to Bajpai, the Rights of Nature offer an opportunity for exploring problems of transboundary rivers' management and for possible cooperation between neighbouring countries.[12] If the river is represented, a more meaningful conversation about its interests would follow. Because then there will be one designated guardian, or a guardian structure, that looks solely and integrally at what the river needs and voices those interests.

That is why Bajpai and other experts are performing extensive research on examples of the Rights of Nature around the world and are investigating what legal personhood for rivers in India could look like.

The ruling of the court in Uttarakhand that awarded legal personality to the Ganga and Yamuna rivers did not change anything for the rivers, as a higher court stayed the ruling. This shows that a ruling recognising the Rights of Nature by a (lower) court is not always final. At this point, the Rights of Nature mean nothing to the Ganga and Yamuna rivers: the judges' rulings have not resulted in laws and policies implementing those rights. And yet, this case is often cited by the Rights of Nature movement. The ruling put rights for rivers on the map, and now people all over the world are exploring what this might mean for rivers in other countries.

The ruling on the legal personality of rivers fits within a remarkable trend in India. Several of its courts have ruled on the rights of non-human entities. In 2017, the High Court of Uttarakhand granted rights to the glaciers Gangotri and Yamunotri, as well as to rivers, forests, lakes, water bodies and even the air. In 2019, judges elsewhere ruled on the legal personality of Hindu idols, as mentioned earlier, and in 2018, the High Court of Uttarakhand granted rights to the entire animal kingdom. In 2020, other judges declared Lake Sukhna a living being, with rights equivalent to those of a person.

In 2022, the Madras state court ruled that living 'Mother Nature' should be a legal subject with rights of its own. Judge Sundaram Srimathy noted that nature should have basic rights to live, be safe, and be maintained. Declaring that particular natural entities have legal status helps to promote the health and wellbeing of the rest of nature. Given these recent developments, it is interesting to note that so far there have been no further moves regarding legal status for the Ganga and the Yamuna rivers.

The discussion on the Rights of Nature is alive and thriving in India, despite the fact that the ruling on the legal personality of the Ganga and the Yamuna rivers was overturned. It is a good thing that judges in India are speaking out on the Rights of Nature, but in practice these rulings have not yet made a real difference in the protection of nature. Hopefully, studies and actions like those of Bajpai will motivate citizens to stand up for the rights of rivers.

All in all, legal personality for rivers, combined with a guardianship structure that includes citizens, can lead to greater local community participation in river management. We have seen in previous examples that a strong call from society can move politics. The recognition of the Rights of Nature cannot happen without the education and participation of local communities.

⤙ 6 ⤚
The Colombian Amazon rainforest has a right to protection

A children's movement for the rainforest

In 2017, environmentalist Gabriela Eslava was living in Bogotá, the capital of Colombia. She was 26 years old at the time. Eslava is passionate about all things related to the environment and she wanted to research deforestation in the Amazon. This vast area is the world's largest rainforest and crosses Colombia, Brazil, Bolivia, Venezuela, Guyana, Suriname, French Guiana, Ecuador, and Peru. Carnivorous plants, pink dolphins, capybaras: the most extraordinary animals and plants are found in this rainforest. Large spaces of the Amazon are unexplored, and new species are still being discovered by scientists.

And yet, this area is seriously threatened. Every day, soccer fields worth of rainforest disappear. Fires are being lit (illegally) to clear land for soy production. Century-old trees are being cut down for timber production. Those who live in the forest, from endangered animals to Indigenous peoples, are being chased from their homes. In Colombia, where the Amazon is as large as the area of Germany and England combined, the rainforest is disappearing at an unprecedented rate. This is not only a disaster for humans, animals, and the rest of nature, it also negatively affects the global climate.

Whereas the rainforest used to absorb huge amounts of CO_2 through trees and plants, it now emits as much or even more CO_2 than it can absorb due to deforestation and increasing drought. The health of the Amazon is of utmost importance for all types of life forms – and for future generations. That is why Eslava, together with the human rights organisation Dejusticia, began a comprehensive study into deforestation in the Amazon in 2017. She was stunned to find that more greenhouse gases per square kilometre were emitted from the Amazon even than from big cities like Bogotá, where she is from.[1]

During her research, Eslava concluded that the Colombian government was not doing enough to combat deforestation and climate change. This had to change, and she decided to take action. She contacted 17 young people spread across the 17 cities and regions in Colombia that are most vulnerable to the effects of climate change. For example, 8-year-old Aymara Cuevas Ramírez from the city of Itagüí, who was at times unable to attend school because heavy rains and floods blocked the roads. Or 22-year-old Catalina María Bohórquez Carvajal, from the city of Manizales, who experienced drinking water sources drying up in her region due to climate change.[2] Unbeknownst to them, these children would start a movement and initiate a first-of-its-kind lawsuit in Latin America, leading to the recognition of the rights of the Amazon.

Taking legal action

The 25 youngsters, ranging in age from 7 to 26 years old, together with Dejusticia, decided to take legal action. Of course, they had to think of a legal path they could take. 'How can we make a legal case, how can we prove that we have standing – if I am a person that does not live in the Amazon, yet climate change effects are happening in the southern area of my city that are affecting me now and will affect me in the future?' said Eslava. They decided to go with an *acción de tutela*.³ This is a legal action, provided for in the Constitution of Colombia, that any citizen can bring before a judge if they believe fundamental rights are being violated or threatened by the actions or inaction of government agencies. This action allows citizens to claim immediate protection of their rights by requesting a judge to issue a ruling that must be complied with immediately. It is a relatively simple procedure that does not require the involvement of a lawyer.

In their claim, the plaintiffs argued that the Colombian government was not fulfilling its duty to protect the environment. This, they asserted, threatened their fundamental rights to life, health, food, and water. They first took the claim to a court in Bogotá; the court rejected their action. The youngsters understood that this would be a difficult legal process: as Eslava said, 'We were fully aware that this case was difficult to understand for a traditional judge. This was not a traditional damage case.'

After their claim was rejected in Bogotá, the youngsters appealed, and in February 2018 the matter was brought before the Corte Suprema de Justicia, Colombia's Supreme Court for civil, criminal, and labour disputes. The Supreme Court overturned the lower court's decision and declared the *tutela* action admissible. This ruling was exceptional, the judges said, because the collective environmental protection interests in this case affected individual fundamental rights, such as the right to water. Now the case could proceed.

The government failed to stop Amazon deforestation and rising temperatures due to climate change, the 25 plaintiffs claimed. As a result, their future and that of subsequent generations was endangered. They argued that their fundamental rights to life, health, food, water, and a clean and healthy environment were threatened as a result. Moreover, they also claimed that Colombia was not complying with national and international climate commitments.

The Supreme Court verdict came out in April 2018 and ruled in favour of the youngsters: Colombia was not doing enough to combat deforestation and fight climate change. This was well supported by facts. The Instituto de Hidrología, Meteorología y Estudios Ambientales (Institute of Hydrology, Meteorology and Environmental Studies) published quarterly reports on early signs on deforestation which were used by the youngsters as scientific evidence for their case. There was a high probability of 'imminent and serious harm' to present and future generations, the judges said. Deforestation also advances the greenhouse effect. Increasing environmental degradation was an attack on the lives of present and future generations and their fundamental rights.

This is an interesting point in the ruling: not only do today's generations have fundamental rights, but future generations have them as well.

The judges in this case made another consequential remark in their ruling. Not only do present and future generations have rights that must be respected, but the Amazon itself also has rights. The judges based their ruling on an earlier case in Colombia. Following the pollution of the Atrato River, judges ruled in 2016 that the river had rights to protection, conservation, maintenance, and restoration. A guardianship structure had been set up to represent it. The ruling on the Rights of Nature in the Amazon case was not new. Based on the reasoning of this earlier case, the court ruled that the Colombian Amazon also has rights of its own. According to Eslava, 'the judge [in this case] understood that the planet does not belong to us, we belong to the planet. This judge had the power to write that in a decision.' In recognising this, the judges stated that the Amazon itself is entitled to protection, conservation, maintenance, and restoration under the direction of state and regional agencies. These are not the same rights that people have.

Historian Thomas Berry is one of the founders of Earth Jurisprudence, a legal philosophy of how we should interact with the Earth.[4] The idea that nature should have intrinsic rights is reflected in his theory. Berry argues in his books (including in *The Great Work: Our Way into the Future* [1999]) that all members of the Earth community have rights. Rivers have river rights and people have human rights. People should specifically design rights to fit nature's needs. The Rights of Nature are not the same as human rights. And that makes sense, because a river would not benefit from a right to vote, and humans have no use of the right to flow freely.[5]

The case of the Amazon in Colombia shows that human rights and the Rights of Nature go hand in hand. A 2020 report by the UN's Harmony with Nature programme stated:

In the past 50 years, although acknowledgement has grown that human rights are intertwined with the environment in which we live, environmental laws have largely failed to reduce pollution and prevent species and habitat loss on which human rights depend. Recognising the Rights of

Nature in law fills that void and proves complementary to human rights.[6]

In Uganda, the Rights of Nature were incorporated in a National Environment Act in 2019 after advocates argued that the human right to a healthy environment could not be realised unless the health of nature itself was also protected. A clean and healthy environment is in the interest of all life on Earth.

Government, act now!

The Amazon rights ruling formed an important building block for the development of the Rights of Nature in Colombia. Following the 2018 Amazon case, judges determined that the Otún, Pance, Quindío, Magdalena, Cauca, Coello, Combeima, Coccora, La Plata, and Fortalecillas rivers are entities with rights of their own. The rights of Lake Tota, Complejo de Páramos Las Hermosas National Park, Los Nevados, and Isla de Salamanca were also recognised by judges as entities with their own rights. In the summer of 2024, the non-profit Amar Madre Tierra Foundation filed a case on behalf of a tropical dry forest, jaguars, and macaws against mining operations that violate the Rights of Nature. A movement for the Rights of Nature has taken shape since the 25 children who brought the Amazon lawsuit set a precedent in Colombia.

Following the ruling, Colombian authorities were given four months to create an action plan to stop deforestation in the Amazon. The government authorities, including the Ministry of Environment and Sustainable Development, had to work with the plaintiffs, the general population, and scientific organisations to create an 'intergenerational pact for the life of the Colombian Amazon'. This was to include measures aimed at stopping deforestation and reducing greenhouse gas emissions. Action also had to be taken at a local level. For example, the municipalities surrounding the Amazon had to revise their *Planes de Ordenamiento Territorial* (a type of land management plan) within five months and create an action plan to combat deforestation. Regional environmental authorities also had to draw up an action plan to combat deforestation.

Internationally, the ruling in this Colombian case was endorsed as one of the most high-profile climate cases ever adjudicated. The lawsuit was a first of its kind in Latin America and triggered a storm of climate cases around the world, in which individuals held their governments responsible for the consequences of climate change. Michael Gerrard, director of the Sabin Center for Climate Change Law at Columbia University in New York, stated that this is 'one of the strongest rulings on the environment that any court in the world has ever made'.[7] The Minister of Environment at the time of the Amazon case, Luis Gilberto Murillo Urrutia, said in a response to the court's ruling in the case of the 25 youngsters that granting rights to the Amazon is something exceptional. It entails a responsibility, not only for the state, but for all of Colombian society to act.[8]

The future of the rights of the Amazon

Yet one year after the case, Dejusticia reported that little progress had been made. In May 2018, the Ministry of Environment and Dejusticia joined forces to draft an action plan against deforestation in the Amazon. The 25 plaintiffs also met around that time to draft the intergenerational pact. But there were still no concrete action plans. Although the government organised several workshops to draft an action plan combating deforestation, there was only an incomplete first version one year later.

The intergenerational pact for the life of the Colombian Amazon has been delayed and a timeline and budget have still not been agreed. Of the 81 municipalities around the Amazon that needed to revise their land management plans, only 14 submitted revised plans. None of those plans came up with concrete strategies to stop deforestation, according to Dejusticia.

By acting in this manner, the Colombian government did not comply with the judges' ruling. In fact, Dejusticia reported that deforestation in the Colombian Amazon has increased.[9] Therefore, in April 2019, the 25 youngsters petitioned the Superior Tribunal of Bogotá to declare that Colombia had not complied with the ruling. They also launched a petition, for which they collected 162,000 supporting signatures.[10] Because the Colombian government is not taking action, people are taking the matter into their own hands. In the summer of 2024, over 1,500 people gathered in Bolivia for an international forum. During this event, a Declaration of the Rights of the Amazon was created. This declaration recognises, among others, that 'the Amazon has a right to life, to be free from contamination... Human beings are responsible for promoting and defending the rights of the Amazon.'[11] Recognising the Amazon as a subject of rights is essential for its protection and restoration because, according to the declaration, this will provide a robust legal framework to safeguard its ecological integrity and uphold the rights of the Indigenous peoples and local communities that depend on it. When Colombia hosted the Conference of the Parties (COP) in Cali in 2024, the declaration was submitted to the authorities of Brazil and Colombia. It declared that 'following the 2018 ruling of the Colombian Supreme Court of Justice, which recognised the Amazon as a subject of rights, now is the time to raise our voices and demand rights for the Amazon'.

Action on deforestation in the Amazon seemed to be progressing slightly better in 2025. In February, the Minister of Environment and Sustainable Development presented the preliminary report on deforestation. Despite challenges, deforestation was reduced by 40 per cent during the period 2022 to 2024.[12] Community engagement and institutional strengthening seem to be particularly effective. The so-called Deforestation Containment Plan is the current model used. It focuses on partnerships with local communities, environmental policies that promote harmonious coexistence with nature, institutional strengthening, strategic protection by public forces and criminal investigations. But deforestation remains a big challenge. The case of the 25 Colombian youth shows that judges' rulings can lead to interesting legal discussions, but also that it is still a tall order to achieve real results. The ongoing deforestation in Colombia contrasts sharply with the judges' ruling that the Amazon has a right to protection, conservation, maintenance, and restoration. 'We need to go beyond wins on paper,' says Eslava. Things seem to be changing, but the Amazon's right to exist, thrive and evolve is still seriously under threat.

⤙ 7 ⤚
Rights of Mother Earth in the Constitution of Ecuador

Nature versus economy

Just like Colombia, Ecuador has a rich natural environment. In Ecuador, you will find waterfalls, jungles, swamps, mountains, and the famous Galapagos Islands. The country is considered one of the 17 countries with the greatest biodiversity in the world. This natural richness extends to the soil as well. The ground is full of petroleum, gold, and silver. Oil is the engine of Ecuador's economy. In 2024 alone, 475,000 barrels of oil were pumped from the ground. This makes Ecuador one of the largest oil exporters in Latin America.[1]

This is good for the national economy, but terrible for nature. The most vulnerable areas, such as rainforests, are hit hard by extractive activities for economic gain. This also applies to Indigenous peoples, who depend on these ecosystems for their livelihood. This is not just a matter of survival: for many people, nature is inseparable from their cultural and spiritual values. They feel an intrinsic connection to ancient forests, rivers, and mountains. Destructive activities endanger not only their direct environment, but also their way of life.

It has been really important for the (Indigenous) peoples of Ecuador that things change in a fundamental way – not just for nature, but also for themselves in regard to social equality, discrimination, and the lack of representation at the government level. For years, they have fought for participatory and inclusive policies that recognise Ecuador's diversity and the culture of its Indigenous peoples.

A key item on the national agenda in Ecuador in the mid-2000s was the drafting of a new Constitution – the highest law in the country.

A new Constitution

To lead this process, a Constitutional Assembly was formed, composed of experts and political representatives from diverse backgrounds. They worked on various issues to write a new foundational text for the country. Indigenous Ecuadorians were given a seat at the table in this process.[2]

A key guiding principle for the new Constitution became *sumak kawsay* (in Spanish *buen vivir*), or 'the good life'. This concept, rooted in the worldview of the Quechan people of Ecuador, Peru, and Bolivia, emphasises life in harmony with nature and the community.

Sumak kawsay stands in contrast to the concept of development in the West. Western notions of development tend to focus on economic growth, but *sumak kawsay* is about community, culture, and ecological balance. Under *sumak kawsay*, humans strive to live in harmony with the rest of nature.[3] There is a deep respect for Pacha Mama (Mother Earth), and recognition of the intrinsic value of all beings.

Another important aspect of *sumak kawsay* is reciprocity. This applies not only to humans, but also to their relationship with rivers, forests, and animals. 'According to this concept, people not only give and take with each other, but also with nature,' says Dorine van Norren, diplomat and scientist, who researched this concept in Ecuador. 'For example, when Indigenous peoples drink something, it is normal for them to throw a little water on the ground to give Mother Earth something to drink. None of what we get from the Earth is taken for granted. We are the keepers of nature.'[4]

* * *

Alberto Acosta, a former Minister of Energy and Mining with a deep commitment to environmental justice, became president of the Constitutional Assembly. Upon his appointment, he made a strong case for including the Rights of Nature in the Constitution. He advocated enshrining these rights in the Constitution to establish a new path for nature, comparing the Rights of Nature to the recognition of rights for women and enslaved people.[5]

The Constitutional Assembly responsible for drafting the proposed amendments to the Constitution was also inspired and supported by CELDF, the same environmental organisation that helped Tamaqua Borough and Pittsburgh draft their Rights of Nature clauses. Now they helped draft the new chapter seven of the Ecuadorian Constitution, which is devoted entirely to Rights of Nature. In the new Constitution, Pacha Mama is considered the place where life takes place and is passed on. Mother Earth has the right to integral respect for her existence and for the preservation and regeneration of her life cycles, structure, functions, and evolutionary processes. She also has the right to restoration.

Ecuador's proposed new Constitution, including the Rights of Nature, was adopted on 28 September 2008.[6] In the referendum on the new Constitution that followed, the proposal received the support of over 64 per cent of the voters. That makes it sound as if the majority of citizens supported the inclusion of Rights of Nature, but the reality is more nuanced. Referendums are inherently political. Voter decisions often reflect broader sentiments about the political climate. Ultimately, the voters did not just vote for the Rights of Nature, which eventually became a historic and globally significant move. The Rights of Nature formed just one chapter in a broader constitutional package that promoted change.

Nature and animal rights

Ecuador is the first country in the world to recognise the Rights of Nature in the Constitution. To guarantee the Rights of Nature, the Constitution requires the state to take precautionary measures. The government must protect these rights proactively, for example by restricting activities that threaten nature with extinction, destroy ecosystems, or alter natural cycles. In practice, this is extremely challenging. Ecuador's economy is dependent on the extraction of raw materials, for which nature often has to make way.

In Ecuador, all 'individuals, communities, peoples and nations' can stand up for the Rights of Nature. This can be done in court at the local, provincial, or national level. This set-up is different from what happens in Aotearoa/New Zealand, for example, where guardians who are appointed under law and operate under a co-governance model are authorised to speak on behalf of the legal person: the Whanganui River.

Moreover, in Ecuador the power to stand up for the Rights of Nature is not just limited to citizens. Foreigners are also able to bring actions. In 2011, two Americans who lived along the Vilcabamba River started a lawsuit on its behalf. The fact that no one is excluded, and everyone can stand up for nature's rights seems, at first glance, to be fair. But who among ordinary citizens has the time, energy, and financial resources to file lawsuits? Isn't it really only possible for the wealthy to file expensive lawsuits on behalf of nature?

The new Constitution does not describe what the term 'nature' means. Because this is such a broad concept, and because anyone can file a lawsuit on behalf of nature, there have been quite a lot of Rights of Nature cases in Ecuador. For example, there have been lawsuits about mining in a cloud forest, the pollution of rivers, the protection of mangrove forests, and the critically endangered condor.

Ecuador's Constitutional Court confirmed in January 2022 that wild animals also fall within the framework of the Rights of Nature. That was the ruling in a case involving the woolly monkey Estrellita, who had been taken from the wild as a baby and had been the pet of the same person for 18 years.[7] Wild animals are not allowed to be kept as pets in Ecuador, so the authorities took Estrellita away and placed her in a zoo. The monkey did not fare well there.

Just before she died, Estrellita's owner started legal proceedings to get her back and have the court declare that her rights had been violated. The court held that those rights had indeed been violated by removing her from her natural habitat in the wild. The court also stated that 'animal rights are a specific dimension of nature rights', 'with peculiarities of their own'. Because animals are part of the ecosystem, individual animals are automatically protected as part of constitutional protections.

The Rights of Nature movement shares many similarities with the animal rights movement. The latter holds the same belief that animals, like the rest of nature, have intrinsic value, and that every animal has the right to life, and to be free from exploitation and suffering. Nature and animal rights can be seen as an extension of each other, although this can raise questions like: if ecosystems are recognised as subjects with rights, why are sentient beings like animals still legally treated as property? The future will show how these movements can further support each other and whether they might be combined. In 2024, Ecuador's Constitutional Court took another bold step by recognising legal rights for coastal marine ecosystems, ensuring their protection and restoration. This landmark decision extends the nation's 2008 Rights of Nature Constitution to marine environments for the first time. The ruling emphasises the intrinsic value of these ecosystems and mandates government action to safeguard them from threats like overfishing and industrial activities. The court emphasised that industrial fishing activities must be restricted within an 8-nautical-mile exclusion zone to preserve the life cycles and evolutionary processes of marine ecosystems. This sets a powerful precedent for environmental protection but also for the biodiversity found in these marine environments.

Developments in the courtroom

What is special and unique about Ecuador is that it adheres to a civil law tradition. This means that written law is one of the main sources of law. But, because the Ecuadorian Constitution offers little explanation regarding the application of Rights of Nature, its interpretation has been developed through the courts. Some environmental laws in Ecuador do mention Rights of Nature, but in doing so merely repeat the provision in the Constitution without elaborating. Judges have taken on that task by ruling on how the Rights of Nature should be applied.

In 2008, the first judges appointed to the Constitutional Court ruled a handful of times on the Rights of Nature, but their rulings were criticised as being too political and of poor legal quality. The composition of the court was subsequently changed and, since 2019, consists of nine magistrates. These judges have issued multiple rulings on the Rights of Nature, one of the most recent rulings in 2024. According to Hugo Ivan Echeverría, an Ecuadorian lawyer who works with Rights of Nature on a daily basis, the rulings of this court are clearly of a high legal standard. The judges apply constitutional provisions already enshrined in the Constitution to the application of Rights of Nature.

More than 64 lawsuits dealing with Rights of Nature have been filed in Ecuador. These cases were not always won easily. Rights of Nature is a new concept for judges and lawyers, and they did not always know how to put it into practice. But over the years, Aotearoa/New Zealand and other countries have come to recognise the Rights of Nature and examples of its application have started to accumulate. Judges in Ecuador have been able to refer to such practices in their rulings, building understanding of how Rights of Nature are to be applied. Interest in this topic is growing around the world.

The evolution of the Rights of Nature in Ecuador becomes apparent when you look at the difference between the rulings in the Condor Mirador project lawsuit of 2013, and the Los Cedros cloud forest case, eight years later.

The Condor Mirador project

In southeastern Ecuador lies the Cordillera del Condor mountain range. This area is humid, hot, and tropical. It is one of Ecuador's so-called biodiversity hotspots, with many rare plant and animal species. For example, there are more than four thousand vascular plant species, beautiful plants with a vascular bundle through which they transport water. Scientists are fascinated by the area. New species are still being discovered, and there is a great deal we do not yet know about the area and its inhabitants.

But when you realise that large amounts of copper, gold, and silver are also found in the Cordillera del Condor, you know what comes next. In March 2012, the Ecuadorian government entered into a contract with a foreign mining corporation. The government granted this corporation an environmental permit and permission to operate in the area for the next 60 years. That permit was granted for the so-called Condor Mirador project, which would take place in the middle of the fragile Cordillera del Condor ecosystem. The mining project required the removal of 2,895 hectares of forest. Technical reports showed that the dams that needed to be built for mining were dangerous and carried a high risk of collapse. The Cordillera del Condor ecosystem would be sacrificed for economic gain.

The report that the corporation prepared for this project acknowledged this huge risk. A consulting firm hired by the corporation conducted an environmental impact assessment and found that several species of amphibians and reptiles could become extinct because of the mining activities. The fragile habitats on which their lives depend would be destroyed.

Water sources would also be polluted. Still, the permit was granted.

A group of environmental and human rights organisations, Indigenous peoples from the region, and local communities joined forces to file a lawsuit to stop the mining project. They sued the Ministry of Commodities, the Ministry of Environment, and the foreign mining corporation.[8] The substance of their argument was that the Rights of Nature, the human right to water, and the right to life in the Ecuadorian Constitution would all be violated by this project.

The plaintiffs asked the Ecuadorian government to revoke the permit because, under Article 73 in the Constitution, the government must take preventive measures to limit activities that threaten nature with extinction, destroy ecosystems, or alter their natural cycle. The precautionary principle is clearly stated and, according to the Constitution, projects like this should be stopped before they take place to protect nature. This is especially the case if the permit itself already states that the project would have a devastating effect on nature.

It seemed a clear-cut case. The Rights of Nature would be violated by the activities of large-scale mining. However, we must remember that this case took place in 2013, when the Rights of Nature had only been incorporated in the Constitution for five years. There was no guidance as to how Rights of Nature should be applied.

In February 2013, the judges in Quito, the capital of Ecuador, immersed themselves in the case. They concluded that the Rights of Nature were not compromised by means of this project. The reason given was that the permits had already been granted, and thus, in their view, the environmental requirements had been met *de facto*. The permits had been granted by the competent authorities and were therefore automatically legally valid. Thus, according to the judges, the Rights of Nature had already been taken into consideration.

This reasoning is based on a false assumption. If a permit is granted because it meets the standards of current environmental law, it does not necessarily mean that the Rights of Nature are respected.

The case was very sensitive. Environmentalists who campaigned against mining were not safe. They were driven from their homes, stalked, harassed, and even murdered. This was also the case with the well-known Condor Mirador opponent and leader of the Indigenous Shuar community, José Isidro Tendetza Antún. He stood up for the rights of his community and the Rights of Nature.

In 2014, a few days before Antún was scheduled to travel to the United Nations Climate Summit in Lima to complain publicly about the Condor Mirador project, he was reported missing. Shortly before he went missing, his house had been burned to the ground. A few days later, Antún's body was found along the bank of a river. He lay tied with ropes, clearly tortured, in an unmarked grave.[9] People from his community suspected that this was directly connected to his campaign against mining. This terrible example is but one of a series of attacks on defenders of human and environmental rights in Ecuador.

Today, the handling of the lawsuit against the Condor Mirador project is strongly criticised in light of the development of Rights of Nature in Ecuador. After all, compliance with (environmental) permit procedures does not necessarily mean there has been compliance with Rights of Nature.[10]

The Los Cedros cloud forest

Eight years later, the courts did rule in favour of the Rights of Nature in a case concerning the Los Cedros cloud forest. Located on a steep mountainside, this forest is home to plants and animals found nowhere else. Think spectacled bears, dozens of species of orchid, brown-headed monkeys, endangered frogs, and rare birds. It is covered in thick vegetation, has high humidity, and rainfall is heavy. Cloud forests play an important role in the formation of clouds and microclimates and cover just 0.4 per cent of the Earth.[11]

Like the Cordillera del Condor mountain range, this is truly a biodiversity hotspot. The area is officially a protected forest but was nevertheless seriously threatened by mining plans. In 2017, a national mining company obtained mining concessions and environmental and water permits for over 68 per cent of the forest area. The company wanted to extract metals, such as copper and gold, from the rich soil at the expense of the habitat of all those rare spectacled bears, endangered frogs, and birds.

In 2018, the Cotacachi community, which lives in the area surrounding the forest, protested against the mining permits in Los Cedros in court proceedings. They held the company and the Ministry of Environment responsible for the permits that had been issued. Their argument was that legal assurances were not being respected because the Los Cedros cloud forest enjoys a protected status and should therefore be protected against this type of destructive activity.

They also cited an article from the Constitution stipulating that local communities must be consulted in advance of mining plans. This had not been done. The judge responded mockingly. 'You are talking about Rights of Nature that are in the Constitution. Who should we judges ask questions about the violation of these rights? The trees? The birds?'[12] The judge also said that prior consultation with local communities was not required, since people did not live *in* the protected forest but nearby. With that, the procedure was dismissed.

After this setback, the community took the case to a provincial court, and there they were more successful. These judges conceded that local residents had not been consulted and that the Constitution had not been respected. However, they said nothing about the protected status of the forest and the Rights of Nature. Therefore, the plaintiffs took the case to Ecuador's Constitutional Court to obtain the explicit recognition of the Rights of Nature.

The Constitutional Court declared that the previously granted mining concessions and environmental permits had violated three different rights enshrined in the Ecuadorian Constitution: the Rights of Nature, the right to water and a healthy environment, and the right of local communities to prior consultation. The judges found that no threatening activities, such as mining, should be allowed in the protected Los Cedros Forest, because that could violate the Rights of Nature. To determine when an activity violates these rights, the judges applied a two-step test:

1 First, the court looked at the existence of a potential risk of severe and irreversible damage to nature;
2 Second, it considered the lack of scientific certainty about the negative impacts of an activity.

These two criteria can be applied to future activities that could violate the Rights of Nature. Mining and other destructive activities that could violate the Rights of Nature are now prohibited in this forest. The permits for mining were revoked by the court. This ruling could set a major legal precedent in Ecuador. Ecuadorian lawyer Echeverría said about the Los Cedros case: 'Animals were preferred to mining, an important source of income for Ecuador. Never before has a court taken this step.'[13]

In 2024, a cultural development demonstrates that the Rights of Nature is also extending to cultural and social domains. A legal petition was filed by the More Than Human Life project to recognise the Los Cedros cloud forest as the co-creator of a musical composition titled 'Song of the Cedars'. The petition argued that the forest's sounds, presence, and ecological rhythm were an integral part of the creative process and therefore deserved recognition as a moral author. The decision is still pending, but it demonstrates that the debate over nature as a rights-holder is extending to other domains.[14] Even earlier, the Museum of the United Nations recognised nature as a musical artist and came up with a special construction to raise money for nature conservation. Artists who use nature sounds can now include 'NATURE' as a contributing artist on Spotify. Then 50 per cent of the royalties from these tracks go to nature conservation. Also, 70 per cent of the royalties of songs that are added to the category of 'NATURE' are donated to charity. Through this initiative, the museum hopes to raise $40 million within four years.[15] If the sounds come from nature, why shouldn't nature benefit from them too?

A paradigm shift

The fight for the Rights of Nature in Ecuador seems to be succeeding. Echeverría says that the Rights of Nature have proven much more effective in nature protection than environmental laws. One thing learned during the past 16 years of their application is that the Rights of Nature are backed by science. This was the case with Los Cedros, but also in other cases, as engineers, ecologists, zoologists, and other experts were involved in court cases on the Rights of Nature. Rather than relying solely on legal and technical norms established by existing environmental legislation, judges have started to ask different questions. What does it mean for ecosystems to have a right to exist, thrive, and evolve? By asking these questions, judges automatically invite a multidisciplinary approach to understanding what nature needs. Interestingly, this means that science can use the Rights of Nature as a vehicle to advocate for its needs. Professor Stone predicted this change would happen in his 'Should Trees Have Standing' article in 1972: 'A court that sees the river as having a legal right will see a different river from one that does not.' Whereas the Rights of Nature were merely a vague legal concept when they were introduced in 2008, judges have now transformed them into applicable norms in line with human rights and environmental law.[16]

Despite these legal advances, Ecuador continues to face profound challenges in ensuring a balance between human activities and nature conservation and protection. The cases in which the Rights of Nature were addressed are about the extraction of natural resources, hydroelectricity, and fishing in protected areas. As a result, resistance is beginning to mount among powerful and wealthy corporations that have an interest in exploiting nature. The best lawyers in the country are hired by the big companies to litigate against the Rights of Nature. It is an expected reaction, and one predicted in 1972 by Christopher D. Stone, the professor who advocated for Rights of Nature. Yet, the Constitution allows for both: respect for nature's rights *and* development by means of extraction and human activities. This is a challenge and a work in progress, as a balance will always have to be sought between human activities and the conservation of nature.

A so-called paradigm shift is always accompanied by the loss of power or influence on the part of established, powerful parties. When nature gains a legal status, the relationship between humans and the rest of nature changes. Nature acquires a new status and suddenly becomes a stakeholder that has to be taken seriously. This may not be in the interest of those working in extractive industries that exploit nature for human gains.

Constitutional proposals around the world

To date, Ecuador is the only country in the world that has included the Rights of Nature in its Constitution. There seemed to be a slight chance that this would change when citizens of Chile were allowed to vote on a new Constitution in September 2022. The proposal for the new Constitution, which was to replace dictator Pinochet's old one, included the recognition of nature as a rights-bearing subject. Nature in Chile, as in Ecuador, would have the right to protection and respect for its existence, the right to regenerate, and to the preservation and restoration of ecological functions. This would include natural cycles, ecosystems, and biodiversity.

The text of the proposed new bill was more far-reaching than Ecuador's Constitution. It also dealt with (the feelings of) animals, climate change, and the protection of oceans. Ultimately, it did not come into effect, as 62 per cent of the more than 15 million citizens voted against it.[17] This came as no surprise: there was a lot of unrest in the country and, according to a Chilean lawyer, a lobbying effort by powerful parties was taking place to undermine the Rights of Nature campaign and the new Constitution.

Currently, there are constitutional proposals for the Rights of Nature in other countries, such as Sweden, Colombia, the Netherlands, and Germany. Ecuador's example shows that the inclusion of Rights of Nature in the Constitution offers a solid foundation, but that concrete guidance and standards for its implementation are needed. The mere recognition of the Rights of Nature in the Constitution is not enough. Ecuador lacks laws, regulations, and policies that provide practical guidelines for the application of the Rights of Nature. The Constitution has not set up a guardianship structure, as was done in Aotearoa/New Zealand, to guarantee observance of the Rights of Nature. Instead, any person in Ecuador can bring a case regarding the violation of the Rights of Nature. This may sound fair, but there is a lack of support, particularly financial support, for citizens who want to do this.

Nevertheless, there is a rich history of cases on the Rights of Nature in Ecuador. Judges have filled the voids left by legislators and applied and further developed the understanding of the Rights of Nature. In that respect, it is interesting to think about the role of judges. Are they not assuming the role of politicians when creating guidelines for the implementation of the Rights of Nature? Laura Burgers, associate professor at the University of Amsterdam, holds a PhD on the democratic legitimacy of lawmaking in climate justice cases. In principle, a judge should only apply the letter of the law in a case, she explains. But sometimes a standard is left deliberately vague, and the judge can interpret it in a context. The law is always changing and must be interpreted so as to keep up with the times. The judges are the legal experts on the Constitution, whereas legislators are political experts on policy matters.[18] One might wonder whether judges are, in the end, the best actors to establish guidelines on the Rights of Nature in line with existing human rights and environmental laws – rather than the politicians, who are often driven by short-term interests. This is an interesting perspective on the developing and changing legal context.

Ultimately, we see that the evolution of these rights depends not just on bold judges or visionary laws, but also on movements, musicians, and communities that insist nature is not property but alive.

↠ 8 ↞
Spain is leading the way in Europe with rights for a lagoon

'A green soup'

The movement advocating for the Rights of Nature is also beginning to gain ground in Europe. Citizens are standing up for rights for rivers in England and moot courts have been held in Sweden to explore, in a fictional context, the possible application of rights for Lake Vättern. In Northern Ireland, the Rights of Nature was recognised as a guiding principle by two local districts in 2021. In the Netherlands, multiple municipalities have put the Rights of Nature on their political agendas. The list of European countries researching and launching Rights of Nature initiatives is growing. But the real frontrunner, when it comes to the Rights of Nature in Europe is Spain.

Spain was the first European country to take a big leap and embed the legal personality of the Mar Menor in a national law. The Mar Menor ('minor sea' in Spanish) is a lagoon in the province of Murcia in the southeast of the country. With an area of 135 square kilometres, a long coastline, and depths of up to 7 metres, it is the largest saltwater lagoon in Europe.[1] Only a narrow strip of land separates the lagoon from the Mediterranean Sea. The salt water of the Mar Menor feeds the surrounding region, creating a diverse variety of habitats:

from dunes and swampy marshes to volcanic islands and lush plains.

The area is home to a large number of species, some of which are endangered – the eel, for example, which is critically endangered. Between 2012 and 2017, the number of seahorses, once abundant in the Mar Menor, declined by as much as 90 per cent.[2] And it's not just for the sake of biodiversity that its saltwater is of great importance: the lagoon is a real tourist attraction. People come from all over the world to enjoy the shallow and crystal-clear waters and spend their summers there.

These days, the water is far from crystal clear. In fact, tourists have been strongly advised against swimming in it. Agricultural activities in the region have been dumping tons of nitrate and other waste in and around the Mar Menor for years. Dumping is not the only source of pollution: the lagoon is seriously threatened by pollution from local mining, uncontrolled urban planning, poor urban sewerage, intensive agriculture, pig farming, and other forms of harmful human activities.

On paper, the Mar Menor enjoys several protected statuses. It is a Natura 2000 site, included in the Ramsar List of Wetlands of International Importance, designated as a Specially Protected Area under the Barcelona Convention, and partially recognised as both a regional park and a protected landscape under various regional regulations. In practice, however, in the past 25 years, environmental laws have failed to ensure that the lagoon is adequately protected.

The only organisms that benefit from the polluted water are algae. They thrive in the thick, green soup, which was how the waters of the Mar Menor came to be described. It was in 2016 that the Mar Menor was first referred to as a 'green soup' by scientists. Over 85 per cent of the seagrass had died off. The severity of the situation became clear again in 2019. The temperature lingered around 40° Celsius for days. The water stank and a tragedy unfolded on the shores of the lagoon: a total of 3 tons of dead marine animals washed up on the beach. The thick green algae soup blocked the sunlight and thousands of fish suffocated due to the resulting lack of oxygen. It was an unprecedented ecological disaster. And it was not just life in the lagoon that suffered: tourists stayed away and real estate prices in the region plummeted.

Meanwhile, in the 2019/20 academic year, a group of eager law students gathered at the University of Murcia. They were to work on a so-called *law clinic*, a legal project in which students can gain practical experience by engaging with clients or by working on a specific legal assignment. This year, the students got to sink their teeth into an exciting new research project on the possibility of attaining legal personality for the Mar Menor. The research group was led by Professor of Philosophy of Law, Teresa Vicente Giménez.

It was a project that resonated strongly with the students. 'I am from the region and have always lived next to the Mar Menor,' Rocío García Martínez, one of the initiative's project coordinators, told Spanish newspaper *El País*. 'When I was a little girl, I sailed and could look down and see the fish at the bottom of the lagoon. Now the water is green and brown, and you can't see anything. I decided to get involved in defending the lagoon when I saw the beach full of dead fish in 2019.'[3]

By May 2020, the research was complete. The students proposed publishing an opinion piece in the local newspaper *La Opinión Murcia*. Together with their supervisor, they wrote an article arguing that the Iniciativa Legislativa Popular (ILP) is the best way to establish the legal personality of the Mar Menor. The Constitution of Spain describes the ILP as a mechanism by which citizens can propose a new law to parliament. Conditions apply that are set out by regulations. At least 500,000 signatures are required in support of the proposal. There are limitations – for example, proposals by citizens cannot deal with tax law or international provisions – but a proposal to make the Mar Menor a legal entity is allowed within this mechanism.

Another environmental disaster

The students tried to solidify their initiative at various political levels. At first, the ILP to recognise legal personality for the Mar Menor and its basin at a regional level was presented in the municipal plenary session of Los Alcázares (a municipality of the Mar Menor), where the proposal was approved by an absolute majority in the summer of 2020. That seemed like a major win, although it was later not admitted for processing in the Assembly of the Autonomous Community of the Region of Murcia because the assembly declared itself incompetent. Towards the end of July 2020, a promotional group made up of eight people presented the ILP – now national in scope – in Madrid. The legal text of both proposals, the regional or municipal ILP and the national ILP, was drafted by Professor Vicente and colleagues.

The initiators knew they would have to go to the Spanish parliament. This was a big project. According to the conditions of the ILP, the initiative required 500,000 supporting signatures, all of which had to be obtained within a nine-month period – quite a job. Due to the Covid-19 pandemic, the initiators had difficulty in getting out into the streets to collect signatures from people who lived in the vicinity of the Mar Menor, which complicated matters. Digital signatures did not qualify. Just over a year later, in August 2021, they had only collected around 300,000 supporting signatures. They were given a three-month extension to collect the remaining 200,000 signatures needed.

And then another environmental disaster occurred. Again, the newspapers were full of it: thousands of dead fish and other species washed up on the beach of the Mar Menor. This time, a total of over 4.5 tons of suffocated marine animals had to be removed from the beaches of the Mar Menor. Some residents described standing at the edges of the lagoon, on the beaches, watching fish and other sea life jump out of the water, gasping for air, suffocating. The locals were now completely fed up. Over 75,000 people joined forces and, hand in hand, formed a 73-kilometre-long human chain around the lagoon. It was a clear and inspiring rallying call from the citizens to protect the Mar Menor.[4]

This was the final push the initiative needed. Now residents began to come up to the initiators, asking to sign the petition. Even the prime minister of Spain, Pedro Sánchez Pérez-Castejón, signed the petition. In October 2021, the initiators delivered over 639,826 supporting signatures to the Spanish Congress. Foreign media wrote about this revolutionary move and people around the world supported legal personality for the Mar Menor.

According to Professor Vicente, the people in the Mar Menor region have a strong bond with the lagoon. 'The Mar Menor belongs to our identity,' she says. Ultimately, the signatures that had been collected ensured that the Spanish government had to act. In April 2022, the Spanish parliament voted overwhelmingly in favour of the initiative.

Only the right-wing Vox party voted against it. According to them, the initiative was 'a way to create a Soviet Union-like state in the Mar Menor, where even the fish can vote'.[5] They submitted a complaint to the Constitutional Court on the unconstitutionality of the Mar Menor law. Despite their disapproval, the court held that the initiative was in line with legal standards; the initiative was adopted and implemented, after which it was transformed into an official law establishing the Mar Menor as a legal person.

The Mar Menor's rights in law

When the initiative was approved, the exact wording of the law still needed to be reviewed by the Spanish parliament's 'Comisión Transición Ecológica y Reto Demográfico'. This is a committee that researches and writes recommendations on ecological transitions and demographic challenges in Spain. For this case, they looked at Spanish and European laws and regulations, and how the legal personality for the Mar Menor would fit in.

During this process, the committee members ran into legal questions that will be familiar to those who have studied the Rights of Nature. For example, how should they define the boundaries of the Mar Menor – was the legal personality just about the water or also the immediate adjacent area? What kind of rights were to be given to the Mar Menor? And who could best represent the lagoon?[6]

These questions were all answered in the law formally establishing the legal personality for the Mar Menor.[7] In September 2022, the Spanish Senate approved the law, and on its entry into force on 3 October 2022, the Mar Menor became the first European natural area with rights. The purpose of the law is to grant the lagoon its own rights, based on its intrinsic ecological value, to ensure its protection for future generations. As the law's preamble states, 'The lagoon is transformed from a mere object of protection, restoration, and development into an inseparable biological, ecological, cultural and spiritual subject.'

The Mar Menor is defined by law as an area that does not consist just of water. The entire basin, including the adjacent land surrounding the water and the aquifers, up to 1,600 square kilometres in all, are part of the Mar Menor legal entity. The geographical boundaries of the Mar Menor as a legal person were determined by ecologists, geographers, and other experts. This makes sense. Just like the Whanganui River in Aotearoa/New Zealand, the ecosystem was used as the starting point for defining the boundaries of the legal entity. The ecosystem of the Mar Menor does not consist only of the water in the lagoon: all the elements surrounding the water are inextricably interconnected. This is a more holistic approach (based on how nature actually functions) rather than traditional environmental protections, which often define a specific area as falling under protection without taking into consideration that everything is connected.

The Mar Menor now has the right to exist and evolve naturally, the right to protection, preservation, and restoration. How these rights will be implemented remains to be seen but, according to Professor Vicente, this law will transform the

Mar Menor from an 'enslaved person' into a 'citizen'. By giving the Mar Menor legal personality, she hopes that plans for the restoration of the lagoon will be carried out. By recognising the rights of the Mar Menor, international provisions such as the climate goals of the Paris Climate Agreement will also be fulfilled. After all, a healthy lagoon also ensures a better CO_2-absorption capacity. In this way, the rights of the Mar Menor can complement current climate and environmental goals.

Defending the Mar Menor

The law also stipulates who can represent and defend the rights of the Mar Menor, which is important when it comes to fighting pollution. Representation also allows for preventive action. When the government, a legal entity (such as a company), or a natural person (a human being) violates the rights of the Mar Menor, that party can be held liable. Three bodies have been appointed to represent the Mar Menor. According to Eduardo Salazar, Chair of Human Rights and Rights of Nature at the University of Murcia and one of the initiators, 'The Mar Menor and its basin's Tutorship was detailed in the Royal Decree 90/2025, approved by the Council of Ministers on the 11th of February 2025. This recent regulation has established the governance model, the functions and the public–private regime of the legal person called "Mar Menor lagoon and its basin".'

The first body consists of a committee of state and regional public administration delegates and citizens. Initially, it will consist of 13 members, 7 of whom are citizens. This is quite extraordinary. Citizens will now also have a say in the protection of the Mar Menor. The duties of this body are to protect, preserve, maintain, and restore the Mar Menor by overseeing compliance with its rights. In doing so it is supported by the two other bodies.

The second body is the monitoring committee, which consists of the guardians, and protectors of the Mar Menor. It will consist of representatives from the surrounding municipalities of Cartagena, Los Alcázares, San Javier, San Pedro del Pinatar, Fuente Álamo, La Unión, Murcia, and Torre Pacheco. These guardians are appointed for a four-year term by the local municipal councils and will be replaced after each municipal election. They must come from economic, social, or environmental sectors involved with the Mar Menor ecosystem, such as people who work to preserve nature in the Mar Menor. Representatives of agricultural associations are also mentioned as examples of potential guardians in the law. The intention is to give everyone a 'place at the table', even representatives of the sector responsible for polluting the Mar Menor (as long as they have worked to promote the ecosystem of the Mar Menor). The duties of this committee are to disseminate knowledge and (periodic) information concerning (compliance with) the Mar Menor law.

The third body is a scientific committee that will research and report on the ecological status of the Mar Menor. This committee includes scientists and renowned independent experts. Their job is to develop indicators for measuring the condition of the ecosystem and identifying risks, and to formulate appropriate remedial measures and pass these on to the monitoring committee.

Together, these three bodies form the tutorship structure of the Mar Menor. But representing and standing up for the lagoon is not just reserved for these bodies. The law states that any natural or legal person can initiate proceedings before a court or public administration to defend the rights of the Mar Menor. If the claim is honoured, the costs of the proceedings, for example the lawyer's fees, will be reimbursed. In this way, initiating legal proceedings becomes much more accessible.

Access to legal proceedings is provided for. This is a sharp contrast to Ecuador, where the Constitution allows any person to start a proceeding on behalf of the Rights of Nature, but fails to give any further guidance or financial support. Those who violate the rights of the Mar Menor, be it a natural person, a government agency, or a company, can be criminally, civilly, environmentally, and administratively prosecuted and sanctioned in accordance with the relevant regulations. Once the legal system is in place, it will be interesting to follow what the Mar Menor's representatives will do to ensure the rights of the Mar Menor are respected and enforced.

The power of 639,826 signatures

Spain is currently setting up the bodies that will represent the Mar Menor. Due to the polluted state of the lagoon, you can imagine that one of the most important tasks for the coming period will be to ensure that the right to restoration is respected. Previously, in September 2022, the Spanish government approved a grant of millions of euros for reparation of the Mar Menor. Municipalities around the lagoon must invest that money in the sewage network and in the treatment of agricultural run-off so that the Mar Menor becomes less polluted.

According to the law, the government must take immediate action to protect the Mar Menor and its rights. The government must establish policies and initiate action for prevention, early warning, protection, and precautionary measures. All activities that may lead to the extinction of species, the destruction of ecosystems, or the permanent alteration of natural cycles of the Mar Menor must be restricted immediately. Furthermore, organisms and organic materials that may permanently alter the biological heritage of the Mar Menor must be banned or restricted. Citizens must also be educated about the environmental hazards and benefits of protecting the Mar Menor. There must be periodic surveys of the state of the ecosystem. These are clear obligations on the part of the government.

The fact that the legal personality of the Mar Menor was established in response to a strong civil movement is significant. It shows that the government could not ignore the 639,826 supporting signatures and societal revolt. The Mar Menor initiative speaks to the potential of civil activism. The signatures of all those citizens who were fed up with the government doing nothing about pollution ensured that the lagoon now has rights of its own. According to Salazar, the transition of anthropocentrism to modern ecocentrism has started in Europe.[8] The Constitutional Court judgment endorsed Law 19/2022 granting the Mar Menor and its basin legal personhood, and confirmed that there is space for the Rights of Nature in the Spanish legal system using a dynamic interpretation of the Constitution.

This brings us back to a point that is being made in several countries. The fact that so much action is being taken on behalf of the Mar Menor, but not for other endangered natural areas in Spain, such as the Doñana National Park, arouses mixed feelings. Yet, those behind the Mar Menor initiative state that a movement has arisen in Spain since this law came into effect. More local Rights of Nature initiatives are being set up for other natural areas. Because it is not only the Mar Menor that deserves rights, but also other natural areas in Spain. As in Aotearoa/New Zealand, change often starts with legal personality for a singular natural area, where it all began with a forest, followed by a river and then a volcano. The case of Mar Menor also demonstrates that this is a movement that is about more than solely making a legal change. People became involved as a result of their relationship with the Mar Menor, and their identification with it as an important part of their locality. In that sense, the rights of the lagoon also serve as a powerful tool in challenging old paradigms and worldviews of nature as property. A movement is taking a stand in Spain. After the Mar Menor, the River Tins in Galicia, in north Spain, now has recognised rights thanks to public participation and the commitment of local authorities.

Although its advance is slow, the Rights of Nature concept is making a difference. Since the law for the Mar Menor was enacted, there has been a new pressure for environmental authorities around the Mar Menor lagoon. According to Salazar, around 90 per cent of illegal irrigation activities have been stopped. The state will invest more than €400 million to restore the basin and there are three criminal cases where the Mar Menor is being represented by five NGOs as a victim of environmental crimes caused by dumping by farming companies and old mining activities. The Mar Menor has a voice, and it is standing up for its rights.

꙳ 9 ꙳
Love Our Ouse: campaigning for river rights in England

Once called 'England's most underrated river', the River Ouse gracefully meanders through the heart of Sussex, England. Along its course, the Ouse supports a broad range of aquatic life, including threatened fish species like the bullhead, but also ancient woodlands, and lush meadows. 'There is nothing about the River Ouse to make it the best or most beautiful waterway in the country,' writes Greg Dickinson for *The Telegraph*. 'It doesn't have the Turner painting bend of the Thames, the spectacle of the Severn Bore, or the steep valleys of the Wye. But it is charming all the same, and quite perfectly embodies the somnolent, quiet appeal of East Sussex.'[1]

From its source near Lower Beeding in West Sussex, the river journeys approximately 35 miles southward, ending its voyage in the English Channel. Along its shore vital ecosystems and vibrant communities are to be found. But beneath its serene surface lies a narrative of environmental challenges, not uncommon to England's rivers, and a growing movement advocating for the river's rights.

Environmental challenges

The River Ouse in Sussex, whose story will be told in this chapter, is not to be confused with the rivers also named

'Ouse' in Yorkshire, Norfolk, Suffolk, and Cambridgeshire. The word 'Ouse' may stem from the Celtic word 'Ūsa', which likely comes from the word *udso-*, meaning 'water'. Besides a name, the river has something else in common with its namesakes. Despite England's rivers having shaped the country's landscape, culture, and ecosystems, they face severe environmental challenges that threaten their vitality.

The challenges that the Ouse faces are those that are found across rivers in the world.[2] Think pollution from agricultural run-off, industrial discharges, and sewage effluents that compromise water quality. Similar to the Mar Menor's problems in Spain, fertilisers have caused the Ouse's water to become overloaded by nutrients, causing algal blooms that deplete oxygen levels and disrupt ecological balances. The natural flow of the river and the life of its inhabitants is compromised by artificial modifications to its course, channelisation, and the construction of weirs. These immediate negative impacts are putting enough pressure on the river as it is, without touching on an even larger problem: climate change. Climate projections for England indicate that rivers like the Ouse will face increased pressure from extreme weather events, including more frequent and intense flooding, longer periods of drought, and higher average temperatures. This will disrupt seasonal flow patterns and water availability, and exacerbate pollution concentrations. The long-term resilience of the Ouse's ecosystem will be harshly tested and potentially undermined.[3]

Data published by the UK Rivers Trust states that no single river in England or Northern Ireland is in good overall health and just 15 per cent of English river stretches reach 'good ecological health standards'. This worrying state of the rivers and the shortcomings of current environmental laws have given rise to a new movement, advocating for a new approach: rights for rivers in the UK.[4] This chapter highlights the fight for the River Ouse in Sussex.

The birth of a Rights of Nature movement

There are thousands of laws that aim to protect nature in the UK, but none have proved sufficient in preventing the current crises around rivers. Besides the lack of enforcement, there is a bigger problem: the lack of community representation in the planning and decision-making processes for the river. If we want things to change for the better, a purely legal approach will not be enough. A grassroots initiative known as 'Love Our Ouse', established in 2022, recognised this. A group of voluntary local residents, nature lovers, and environmental professionals gathered to stand up for the river, with a 'relentless passion and determination'.[5] The idea for a River Charter was first explored in September 2022, during a workshop held as part of the River Festival. During this festival, community members and local activists began to consider a formal rights-based framework for protecting the River Ouse.

A little less than half a year later, on a chilly February day in 2023, the Lewes District Council took a bold next step. Spurred on by early advocacy from Love Our Ouse, the council passed a motion to explore the development of a Declaration on the Rights of the River Ouse, marking the first formal support by a UK local authority for a Rights of Nature initiative. Love Our Ouse was happy, but surprised – they didn't think the motion would pass. One of the conservative leaders stood up before the council and stated that they might as well authorise the research and formation of a declaration, since they had tried everything else to protect and restore the River Ouse.

In passing this motion, the council recognised that the growing global movement of Rights of Nature could serve as a framework for rethinking society's relationship with the river. They believed that a case could be made for reconsidering interactions with the River Ouse in the context of rights which would promote a way for its health and wellbeing to be addressed. The council determined that local communities and other relevant stakeholders would be involved in creating a 'Declaration on the Rights of the River Ouse' for possible endorsement by the council in two years' time.

The River Ouse Charter

Love Our Ouse did not waste any time. On a crisp autumn day, 24 November 2023, they organised a Rights of Rivers summit. Along the river, the leaves had turned golden and brown, while a low winter sun cast long shadows across the Sussex landscape. People gathered – some with notebooks, some with muddy boots, but all with one shared purpose: to speak up for the river. Local farmers and fishers, artists, lawyers, and academics were present. The summit brought all of these stakeholders together to learn about the rights of rivers and explore key implementation mechanisms together.

Then it was time to draft the River Ouse Charter – a document that spells out how the river should be cared for, respected, and protected for generations to come.[6] The charter was created by the steering group of Love Our Ouse, with support from the Environmental Law Foundation, lawyers, and through the public consultation workshops. In the charter, it was recognised that:

> a wide range of organisations are already having a positive impact on the health of the river, utilising to the best of their abilities the often-limited resources available to them. However, there is a need to increase this effort if we are to see improvement which matches the ambition of those at the frontline of positive change especially as the river faces increasing threats across a number of areas.

Through the Rights of Nature framework, the charter calls for the recognition of the river as a living entity, with inherent rights. Its rights are derived from the Universal Declaration on Rights of Rivers, which formulates the 'fundamental' rights of rivers worldwide. The charter states that the River Ouse specifically has rights including 'the right to exist, to flow, to be free from pollution to native biodiversity, to regenerate and restore, to perform essential ecological functions, and to be represented in decisions that affect it.' The right to a say is what makes the charter stand out – it actively calls upon representation of the river and community engagement. 'A purely legal approach is not enough,' says Joshua Levene, director at Love Our Ouse. 'Laws are only going to be implemented when they reflect the values of the community. This charter is a community charter and codifies how we want to relate to the river.'

The charter also proposes a long-term vision: not just the recognition of rights for the river, but active stewardship structures, monitoring frameworks, and mechanisms to ensure the river's voice can be included in future planning and land-use decisions. In that sense, the charter tries to go beyond symbolic recognition and establish an active role for the community to take responsibility for the river. 'The charter calls upon everyone to be a guardian for the river,' says Levene.

From the local community to Lewes District Council

Between 2023 and 2025, in the lead-up to the charter's formal endorsement, community efforts were taken to build support for the rights of the Ouse. The Lewes District Council allowed two years for drafting the charter, and extensive activity was undertaken to get the community involved. For example, the Voice of the River Campaign organised a series of free community events, offering ways for local people to celebrate, learn, and act for the Ouse. From river testing, poets speaking on behalf of the river, talks and debates about the rivers' rights, and arts and crafts, people engaged in all sorts of ways. Love Our Ouse also organised citizen science projects in which local residents play a part in monitoring and reporting on the river's health. In all these efforts, it becomes apparent that a collective identity centred around the Ouse was being formed. As we saw happen in Spain for Mar Menor, if people have a sense of cultural identity around the area in need of conservation this may lead to active community engagement and all local residents will feel a responsibility to uphold the rights regime.

In February 2025, the efforts of the community led to a historic moment. Lewes District Council spoke out and supported the River Ouse Charter. Emily O'Brien, councillor and cabinet member for nature, climate and food systems at the council, said:

It is a very proud moment for me and many others to celebrate this charter for a landmark waterway that has such resonance and influence in Lewes district, and I hope that our council's support will mark another step on the journey to change the conversation, so that one day a change in the law will mean the interests of nature are fully recognised.

Moving forward, this motion could mean creating assemblies where the river's rights are actively considered in council planning. The possibility of appointing river guardians, as explored in the supporting documents, could ensure representation of the river in decisions that affect its wellbeing. The charter will serve as a guiding document, influencing policy decisions, conservation efforts, and community-engagement initiatives. 'This is a historic moment for environmental protection in England,' said Emma Montlake, co-director of the Environmental Law Foundation. 'By supporting the Rights of Rivers, Lewes District Council has set a precedent that could transform the way we safeguard our rivers. The River Ouse is an essential part of the region's ecosystem and cultural heritage – this decision ensures a better future for the river's health and protection.' Now that the charter has been adopted, Love Our Ouse focuses on community engagement, involving different organisations to endorse the charter, and ways of giving meaning to the right of the river to have a say in cases that affect its wellbeing.

Paving the way

The success of the Rights of the River Ouse initiative is deeply rooted in community engagement. Through community action and recognition of the river's rights, it is hoped that the relationship between the community and the river will be transformed, as in many Rights of Nature examples. By acknowledging the river as a living entity, with intrinsic value beyond its utility to humans, a new perspective is promoted. The efforts in community engagement mean that active participation of locals is encouraged in conservation efforts and decision-making processes affecting the river. The movement is open to anyone, including 'recreational users, landowners, farmers and everything in between'. The unity of people coming together for the river is what makes it a strong initiative. As the Love Our Ouse team notes in their press release, '"rights of the Ouse" sets out a renewed relationship between people and nature in which the river's essential rights are clearly articulated alongside humans' duty of care and responsibility to uphold these rights'.[7]

Of course, this movement was met with criticism, as are all Rights of Nature initiatives. There were those who dismissed the idea from the very start. 'Enforcement of these rights might prove challenging, given that existing UK laws don't readily accommodate such a paradigm shift. Conflicts may arise between the rights of the river and pre-existing human rights or property rights,' writes Lasserina Rath.[8] One could also think of the questions that are raised in Rights of Nature movements across the world: Who will speak for the river? Who decides what it needs? Can farmers and local businesses still use the water or adjoining land to the river? The future will bring answers to these questions. Without strong enforcement mechanisms, the charter remains a visionary but symbolic document. It is not legally binding, but one could argue that it is politically and morally binding. For the first time, nature is included in moral and political decision-making, and that represents a systemic shift in river management. And it is being used as a lens for river management plans. In 2025, the annual sewage spill data of the Ouse catchment in 2024 was released. Love Our Ouse used the published data to ask Lewes District Council and the South Downs National Park to review local plans in light of the charter. The Ouse's rights to be free from pollution are constantly infringed, but the community is able to focus attention on the management of the river by invoking the charter.

This community, and their exploration of rights for River Ouse, are not alone. Similar efforts have been undertaken for other rivers in the UK – the Avon, Plym, Don, Cam, Medway, Dart, Exe and Kent. As an overarching piece of legislation on Rights of Nature in the UK seems unlikely to be on the government's agenda any time soon, local movements are taking a stand and presenting opportunities at the local level. The actions of Lewes District Council are exemplary in that regard. The Ouse Charter offers a guideline for other rivers in the UK – blending ecological urgency, community care, a cultural shift in protection, and political will into a new story for rivers in England. 'We are very proud that the first river in the UK to be recognised in its own right is here in Sussex', says Henri Brocklebank from Sussex Wildlife Trust. 'Our rivers need all the support they can get, and this is a great step forward.'

10

Nothing is more powerful than an idea whose time has come

Throughout history, rights have evolved from being reserved for a select few to being extended to more and more entities and beings. Generally, the law lags behind societal and cultural progress. But now, law is at the forefront of the Rights of Nature movement. Looking back and tracing how rights have been won teaches us valuable lessons as we plot the path of the Rights of Nature in the history of societal developments.

Back in time

Anyone who, after reading this book, still thinks the Rights of Nature is a bizarre idea, should picture themselves two hundred years ago. In 1792, the English 'mother of feminism', Mary Wollstonecraft, made a plea for women's rights. She advocated for the educational and social equality of women. Despite the rise of human rights, women were still not allowed to vote. Equal rights for women? Unthinkable!

Just like Professor Christopher Stone with his plea for Rights of Nature, Mary Wollstonecraft faced fierce criticism. Horace Walpole, writer, politician, and the fourth Earl of Orford, tried to silence Wollstonecraft by calling her 'a hyena in a petticoat'. Now, more than two centuries later, the debate about whether women should have rights is a thing of the past.

Historically, rights were initially a privilege of the elite – primarily wealthy, property-owning men. Over time, the scope of rights expanded to include more groups, challenging the notion that only a select few deserved protection and recognition under the law. The struggle for women's rights, the abolition of slavery, and the civil rights movements have all played pivotal roles in this evolution, expanding the circle of justice and equality. The question now is: if we can extend rights to all people and even corporations, why not to nature itself?

The law is constantly evolving according to the most important norms and values of society. The current legal system is representative of an outdated worldview, with humans as rulers over the rest of nature. But as society's values have evolved, so too has the understanding of who and what deserves legal recognition and protection. In an era defined by ecological crises, we are increasingly coming to realise that a green future is vital, not only for ourselves, but also for all other life on this planet. Forests, mountains, rivers, animals: they all have a right to exist. We are not the only beings that depend on the Earth as a home.

Of course, this will take more than just a recognition of rights. As was the case with women or formerly enslaved people, changes in the law are only one of many steps needed to forge a new reality. Just as legal recognition of rights was only the first step in a long fight for equality and justice, recognising the Rights of Nature is a starting point, not the finish line. Recognising the Rights of Nature, however, can be an important first step towards creating an equal balance between humans and the rest of nature. Indeed, in our legal system, rights determine laws and rules, and laws and rules determine behaviour. As Kai Huschke of the CELDF puts it, rights cannot stand alone; they must be integrated into a broader, transformative legal framework. Just as the struggles for women's rights, children's rights, and human rights have been deeply interconnected, the Rights of Nature must not be treated in isolation. Rather than framing these as separate struggles we should build a cohesive framework that recognises the interdependence of all life. Like a forest, where trees communicate through mycelial networks and thrive as a collective organism, our systems of justice must reflect the profound interconnectedness of all life. In nature, animals, plants, fungi, and microorganisms co-create the conditions for life, each depending on the others in life cycles of reciprocity and regeneration. Our legal and political systems should mirror this ecological reality.

For generations, citizens have demanded fair treatment for new groups through establishing rights. This struggle to expand rights – to women, to people of colour, to the LGBTQ+ community, to workers – has shown that societal norms and legal frameworks can change when people demand it. Men had to abide by new laws that protected women's rights. White people had to abide by new rules that protected the rights of people of colour. History proves that a society can change by recognising rights. Consider the Los Cedros case in Ecuador: using the Rights of Nature as a weapon, local communities managed to stop mining in a fragile forest. Devastating activities like mining, the judge said, threaten the rights of the forest.

On the other hand, the Rights of Nature do not always have to be a matter of litigation. As demonstrated by the Whanganui River case in Aotearoa/New Zealand, representing nature through guardians offers a pathway that can enhance dialogue and ensure that the interests of nature are taken into consideration. Court cases are inherently reactive, typically only arising after harm already has occurred, but dialogue can work preventively and ensure that all stakeholders – non-human ones included – are taken into consideration. By institutionalising dialogue as a cornerstone of environmental governance, a culture of prevention rather than reparation is promoted. The Rights of Nature framework offers not only a model for legal redress but also for reshaping human–nature relationships through representation.

It's up to us

Fifty years ago, Christopher D. Stone was ridiculed when he wrote 'Should Trees Have Standing?' But the concept of the Rights of Nature has now become a reality in many places around the world. As English philosopher John Stuart Mill once said, 'Every great movement must experience three stages: ridicule, discussion, adoption.'

The phase of 'adoption' has been reached for the Rights of Nature. It will not be easy; there are still people who think it is a ridiculous idea that nature can have rights. But, just as it was once unthinkable to grant women or people of colour the same legal recognition as men, today we stand on the threshold of a new era where the Rights of Nature could reshape our laws for the better. This global movement cannot be stopped. In this book, I have described a few of the many examples of the Rights of Nature. There are so many stories to tell. Stories of brave citizens, activists, and nature lovers standing up for nature.

Norms and values are shifting, and our Western worldview regarding nature is undergoing a fundamental transformation. For centuries, we have viewed nature as something separate from us – an object to be exploited and controlled. This mindset has deep roots in our history, where nature was treated as property, subject to the whims of those in power. But today, as we face mounting environmental challenges, we are starting to realise that this worldview no longer serves us. We are beginning to understand that our fate is inextricably linked to the health of the planet, and that the wellbeing of nature is essential to our survival.

The hope we find in the Rights of Nature is that its roots start in society. It is a prime example of bottom-up campaigning. In 2024, Ipsos conducted research into attitudes to planetary stewardship and segmentation. Over 22,000 participants from over 20 countries were asked about their opinions, including their views on the Rights of Nature. Over 60 per cent of the respondents support the idea of giving rights to nature in national laws, with only 10 per cent opposed.[1]

What is particularly striking is how younger generations are leading this shift. Children and young people today often view the idea of giving rights to nature as not only logical but necessary. They are growing up in a world where climate change, pollution, and the loss of biodiversity are realities. For them, the concept of nature having rights feels like a natural extension of rights – a way to ensure that future generations will inherit a world where all life can thrive. The 2002 Diné Fundamental Laws of the Navajo people – the first laws to mention the Rights of Nature – recognise this: 'It is the duty and responsibility of the Diné to protect and preserve the beauty of the natural world for future generations.' What older generations may see as radical or unconventional, younger people intuitively recognise as the next step in our evolution as a species. They see the Rights of Nature as a way to restore balance and equity, a necessary correction to centuries of exploitation and neglect.

As a citizen, depending on your country, you can organise a campaign, start a citizens' initiative, or create a petition and take action to draw the attention of politicians and governors to the Rights of Nature. As history has shown, citizens are often the catalysts for meaningful change, as they challenge outdated systems and bring forward new ideas. It is important to research what you can do, as a citizen in your country, to influence politicians. Power to the people.

Ultimately, it is up to politicians and decision-makers to enshrine the Rights of Nature in laws and regulations. We need leaders who are willing to step up and act, as those who championed women's suffrage and civil rights did, even in the face of powerful opposition. It takes guts to do so. Think of Mayor Morrison of tiny Tamaqua Borough: 'Even if I have to appear in court,' he said, 'we're going to protect the community, citizens, and nature.'

That is what is needed: politicians and decision-makers who dare to act, regardless of their own interests. Unfortunately, it rarely happens that political parties come up with an initiative for the Rights of Nature of their own. Just as the civil rights movement and women's rights movements were not initiated by the political elite, it is up to the people, the grassroots movements, to push for change. It is up to the citizens to act. As was the case during the fight for women's rights and the abolition of slavery, real change will follow from citizens rising up against injustice. Petitions demonstrate the will people through thousands of signatures. Citizens collectively launch lawsuits to stop destructive plans by powerful corporations. All over the world people are raising their voices to stand up for nature. In the next chapter, I will tell you how you can join us.

11

Join the movement

We are at the forefront of a legal revolution that is reshaping the way we view our relationship with nature. This legal revolution is supported by a rapidly growing worldwide movement. The recognition of the Rights of Nature is no longer just a romantic idea, as was suggested in the 1970s: it's a powerful force gaining momentum around the world. The best part about this legal movement is that every person has a role to play. You do not need to be a politician, a lawyer, or a city councillor to make a difference. Power lies in the hands of ordinary citizens. Whether through education, advocacy, or grassroots organising, there are countless ways you can take action for the Rights of Nature. Here are some actionable tips to get you started:

- *Educate yourself and others.* The more people understand the legal, environmental, and ethical arguments for the Rights of Nature, the more we can effectively advocate for it. You made a great start by reading this book, but there are countless other ways to engage with Rights of Nature materials. If you prefer to watch films, I recommend the documentaries *Invisible Hand*, which explores grassroots movements for the Rights of Nature in North America, and *I am the River, the River is Me*, which tells the story of the legal personhood of the Whanganui River. The Earth Law Center regularly organises webinars and summer courses on the Rights of Nature. If you are in a position to do so, help give Rights of Nature a place in curricula in schools. This is one of the fastest growing legal movements in the world, but there are hardly any educational programmes dedicated to it. It is an interesting topic for programmes related to law, philosophy, and political science, but even engineering programmes can teach students how nature can be considered and engaged as a stakeholder.

- *Get involved with local actions in your country.* In countries all over the world, you will find grassroots organisations that are pushing for the local recognition of the Rights of Nature. You can join or volunteer with these organisations to contribute to ongoing campaigns and initiatives. Whether you are a lawyer, a scientist, an educator, or an artist, there will be a way to contribute based on your expertise. A lawyer could help with legal cases, a teacher could teach about the growing movement, and an artist could illustrate the voice of nature. You can check if there are organisations working on the Rights of Nature in your country by taking a look at the websites of the Global Alliance for the Rights of Nature and the Eco Jurisprudence Monitor.

- *Sign petitions and participate in campaigns.* Online petitions are one of the easiest ways to show support for the Rights of Nature. There might be ongoing petitions in your country, but you can also express your support by signing international petitions or declarations, for example the ongoing petition 'Be the voice for Mother Earth, say yes to Rights of Nature'. Their goal is to reach

1 million signatures by global citizens to support the recognition of rights for ecosystems. In addition to the Universal Declaration of Human Rights, this petition is asking the United Nations to adopt a Declaration of Rights of Mother Earth.

- *Advocate for policy change.* Reach out to your elected representatives to express support for the Rights of Nature by sending letters and emails, and other forms of communication. Perhaps your local politician has never heard of the Rights of Nature and the possibilities of recognising its principles on a local level. Your voice as a citizen – especially when joined together with a local movement – can positively influence policy decisions. If you speak Dutch, you can consult the toolkit developed by Stichting Rechten van de Natuur (the Rights of Nature Foundation) for help and instructions on Rights of Nature recognitions at local levels and how you can advocate for them as a citizen.

- *Speak on behalf of nature.* Depending on which country you live in, you can use your right to speak as a citizen in local decision-making processes to advocate for nature. Rather than speaking on your own behalf, try speaking on behalf of the forest that is about to be cut down or the river that is about to be polluted. Storytelling is a great way of getting people to think about – and consider – the interests of nature. You can also designate a person within your organisation or implement an organisational model that represents the interests of nature. Check out the toolkit 'Onboarding Nature', for example, which provides the tools for private actors to formalise nature's voice and role in governance structures.

- *Return ownership of the land 'to itself'*. If you are able to do so, you could buy a parcel of land and return ownership of the land in its statutes, giving it back to itself. There are legal provisions that you could include to take it off the market and have an independent structure account for it. Find legal support about how to do so.

- *Support Rights of Nature initiatives through donations*. Financial support is essential to sustain campaigns and legal efforts. Sometimes, it is hard for organisations that advocate for system change to get funding, so your contribution to Rights of Nature campaigns will be much appreciated.

- *Join the Global Alliance for the Rights of Nature*. Join the international alliance for the Rights of Nature so that they can use your membership as evidence of an ever-growing global movement. You can join thematic hubs in which you can engage with people from your region or from a similar background – there are, for example, Youth Hubs, African Hubs, Academic Hubs, and more.

After all, the key lies in citizen movements. This is what the women's rights movement taught us. If it was not for our grandmothers, who took to the streets and called out for the injustice of rights being solely reserved for men, we would not be talking about gender equality as we are today.

The inspiring example of Spain demonstrates just how transformative collective action can be and what power lies in numbers. If the 639,826 signatories of the Mar Menor legal personality initiative had all thought, 'What difference will my single signature make?', they would never have achieved this victory. But together, they stood united – their voices echoing on behalf of their loved Mar Menor – and made history. This is a movement driven by everyday people, each one of us contributing to something far greater than ourselves. When we come together, we can create real, lasting change. So that our future generations, in a hundred years' time, can take a stand and use the laws we enact today to say 'Nature has a right to exist, and you need to respect it.'

Will you join us in this historic fight for the Rights of Nature?

Acknowledgements

I have a lot of people to thank for the process leading up to this book, but I would like to start by thanking editorial director David Castle and the entire team at Pluto Press for their commitment in transforming the message of the Rights of Nature into a book for English audiences.

A heartfelt thank you to my Dutch publisher, Jean Christophe Boele van Hensbroek, publisher at Lemniscaat, and rights manager Robin van der Gaag. Thank you for your encouragement and belief in creating an English version of the original Dutch book. Thank you to Penny Simmers for your support in the English translation.

I also want to thank the entire team and board of my non-profit Stichting Rechten van de Natuur for allowing me the time and space to write this book while so much was happening for the Rights of Nature movement in my home country the Netherlands.

My dear boyfriend, family, and friends: thank you for your support and encouragement while I locked myself away writing this book. Thank you from the bottom of my heart for your support and belief in this book and in me.

Of course, I could not describe the Rights of Nature so well without the feedback of the local experts. Thank you very much for your sharp and constructive feedback: Hugo Echeverría Villagomez, Joshua Levene, Natasha Padbury, Ben Price, Chuck O'Neal, Elizabeth Macpherson, Shrishtee Bajpai,

Eduardo Salazar Ortuño, and Gabriela Eslava Bejarano. All shortcomings and errors in this book remain my own.

It was sometimes quite a challenge to describe worldwide examples of the Rights of Nature without speaking the language or sufficiently understanding the cultural context. I do realise I might have missed – or misunderstood – parts of the processes leading up to the Rights of Nature initiatives. This book is meant to serve as an introduction, based upon which further research into the cultural and legal contexts can be done. I thank all the lawyers, activists, and others whom I interviewed about local laws and challenges. When permitted, I have mentioned them by name in the text. Their work inspires me on a daily basis to continue advocating for the Rights of Nature.

A special thank you goes out to María Mercedes Sánchez, coordinator of the United Nations Harmony with Nature programme. Without María's support over the past few years, since I began my research on the Rights of Nature in 2017, I would never have dreamed of making this my life's mission. I am very grateful to the United Nations network of experts for their work.

My gratitude also goes out to all the initiatives and the people behind them, as described in this book. Advocating for the Rights of Nature is not possible without the broad support of engaged people. The key lies in citizen movements... To all of the other (environmental) organisations and people around the world who are involved with – or are supporting the Rights of Nature – I want to say: thank you and keep using your voice to stand up for nature!

Notes

Introduction

1. Jonathan Watts, 'Could 2024 Be the Year Nature Rights Enter the Political Mainstream?', *The Guardian*, 1 January 2024, www.theguardian.com/environment/2024/jan/01/could-2024-be-the-year-nature-rights-enter-the-political-mainstream.
2. Christopher D. Stone, 'Should Trees Have Standing? Toward Legal Rights for Natural Objects', *Southern California Law Review* 45 (1972), pp. 450–501.
3. Eco Jurisprudence Monitor, 'Political Map', https://ecojurisprudence.org/ (accessed May 2025).
4. United Nations, *Report of the Secretary General: Harmony with Nature*, A/74/236, §129, 26 July 2019.
5. Stichting Rechten van de Natuur, *Initiatieven* (Netherlands), www.rechtenvandenatuur.org/initiatieven (accessed May 2025).

1 Professor Stone and the birth of the Rights of Nature

1. Earthjustice, 'How the Earth got a Lawyer', 20 January 2011, https://earthjustice.org/feature/how-the-earth-got-a-lawyer
2. Harry T. Harvey, Howard S. Shellhammer and Ronald E. Stecker, *Giant Sequoia Ecology: Fire and Reproduction* (Washington, DC: U.S. Department of the Interior National Park Service, 1980), 'Introduction' (updated March 2007).
3. Nathan Masters, 'In the '60s, Disney Almost Built a Ski Resort in Sequoia National Park', *Gizmodo*, 18 February 2014, https://gizmodo.com/a-mountain-disneyland-how-disney-almost-built-a-ski-re-1525286740 (accessed May 2025).
4. Margaret M. McKeown, 'The Trees Are Still Standing: The Backstory of Sierra Club v. Morton', *Journal of Supreme Court History* 43, no. 2 (2018), pp. 189–214.

5. The Holy Bible, Genesis 1, 1:28, 2:15 (New International Version).
6. Biography.com, 'Francis Bacon', www.biography.com/scholars-educators/francis-bacon (accessed June 2025).
7. United Nations, 'Report of the UN Conference on the Human Environment', A/CONF.48/14/Rev.1, 5–16 June 1972, Chapter 1.1.
8. Satish C. Shrasti, 'Environmental Ethics Anthropocentric to Eco-centric: A Paradigm Shift', *Journal of the Indian Law Institute* 55 (2013), pp. 522–530.
9. U.S. Supreme Court, *Sierra Club v. Morton*, 405 U.S. 727, Sec. Int. Opinion by Mr. Justice Douglas, 19 April 1972, pp. 6–7.
10. John M. Naff, 'Reflections on the Dissent of Douglas in Sierra Club v. Morton', *American Bar Association Journal* 58 (1972), p. 820.
11. Winter Wildlands Alliance, 'How NEPA Saved a High Sierra Sanctuary from Becoming a Winter Disneyland', https://winterwildlands.org/how-nepa-saved-a-high-sierra-sanctuary-from-becoming-a-winter-disneyland/ (accessed May 2025).
12. Jim Jansen, 'Vanuit de ruimte zie je dat we de aarde uitputten', *New Scientist* (22 February 2020), www.newscientist.nl/blogs/vanuit-de-ruimte-zie-je-dat-we-de-aarde-uitputten/ (accessed May 2025).
13. Godofredo Stutzin, 'Un imperativo ecológico: Reconocer los derechos de la naturaleza', *Ambiente y Desarrollo* 1, no. 1 (1984), pp. 97–114.

2 People and ecosystems protected from polluters in Pennsylvania

1. Environmental Justice Atlas, 'In Wake of Toxic Dumping: Tamaqua Borough Passes Rights of Nature Ordinance, USA', 25 March 2019, https://ejatlas.org/conflict/tamaqua-borough-passes-ordinance-on-rights-of-nature (accessed May 2025).
2. Cathy Miorelli, 'We the People 2.0 – The Second American Revolution', Community Environmental Legal Defense Fund, 13 October 2016, https://celdf.org/2016/10/cathy-miorelli-people-2-0-second-american-revolution/ (accessed May 2025).

3. Borough Council of Tamaqua Borough, Tamaqua Borough Sewage Sludge Ordinance No. 612, 19 September 2006.

4. Community Environmental Legal Defense Fund, 'Tamaqua Borough, USA', 31 August 2015, https://celdf.org/2015/08/tamaqua-borough/ (accessed May 2025).

5. United States Environmental Protection Agency, 'Hydraulic Fracturing for Oil and Gas: Impacts from the Hydraulic Fracturing Water Cycle on Drinking Water Resources in the United States', Washington, DC: U.S. EPA, EPA/600/R-16/236F, 2016.

6. Madeleine S. Perkins, 'How Pittsburgh Embraced a Radical Environmental Movement Popping up in Conservative Towns across America', *Business Insider*, 9 July 2017, www.businessinsider.nl/rights-for-nature-preventing-fracking-pittsburgh-pennsylvania-2017-7?international=true&r=us (accessed May 2025).

7. United Nations Environment Programme, *Environmental Rule of Law: First Global Report*, Nairobi, 24 January 2019.

8. The 2023 Dutch 'Nitrogen plan' website – www.aanpakstikstof.nl – where this quote appeared (here translated from Dutch by Jessica den Outer) has since been replaced with a new one.

9. City of Pittsburgh, Community Protection from Natural Gas Extraction Ordinance, File #: 2010-0909, Version: 2, §618, 2010.

10. Ben Price, 'In Pittsburgh, a Community Bill of Rights Helped Ban Fracking', *Shareable*, 8 March 2018, www.shareable.net/in-pittsburgh-a-community-bill-of-rights-helped-ban-fracking/ (accessed May 2025).

11. Kristina Marusic, 'Residents in a Densely Populated Pittsburgh Suburb Are Demanding Public Hearings on Two Proposed Fracking Wells', *Environmental Health News*, 18 August 2021, www.ehn.org/pittsburgh-fracking-2654712173.html (accessed May 2025).

12. Kristina Marusic, 'More than 2,000 Studies Show Fracking Harms Pennsylvania Communities', *Environmental Health News*, 13 December 2022, www.ehn.org/pennsylvania-fracking-studies-2669231965.html (accessed May 2025).

NOTES

3 Water bodies appear before judges in Florida

1. U.S. Environmental Protection Agency, 'Saving Water in Florida', factsheet, EPA-832-F-13-006, 2013, www.epa.gov/sites/default/files/2017-02/documents/ws-ourwater-florida-state-fact-sheet.pdf (accessed July 2025).
2. Florida Rights of Nature Network, 'The Right to Clean Water', https://fronn.org/the-right-to-clean-water (accessed May 2025). Red tides are blooms of the microscopic algae *Karenia brevis*, which can kill fish and negatively affect marine life. Growing evidence indicates that they are the result of human activities – pollution caused by agricultural run-off and wastewater.
3. Orange County, '2020 Charter Review Commission', Final Report, Section IV, Question 1.
4. Michaela Haas, 'Does This Water Have Legal Rights?', *Reasons to be Cheerful*, 22 April 2022, https://reasonstobecheerful.world/florida-lake-lawsuit-nature-rights-indigenous-peoples/ (accessed June 2025).
5. Florida Senate, Senate Bill 712 (CS/CS/SB 712), 2020, pp. 82–83.
6. Amy Green, 'Judge Strikes Down "Rights of Nature" Charter Amendment', WUSF Public Media, 12 July 2022, https://wusfnews.wusf.usf.edu/environment/2022-07-12/judge-strikes-down-rights-of-nature-charter-amendment (accessed May 2025).
7. Scott Powers, 'Environmentalists Challenge "Rights of Nature" Preemption in SB 712: The Econlockhatchee River', *Florida Politics*, 2 July 2020, https://floridapolitics.com/archives/345753-environmentalists-challenge-rights-of-nature-preemption-in-sb-712/ (accessed May 2025).
8. Complaint, *Wilde Cypress Branch and others v. Beachline South Residential LLC and the Florida Department of Environmental Protection*, Filing #125602282, Circuit Court of the Ninth Judicial Circuit, Orange County, 26 April 2021.
9. Florida Right to Clean Water, 'Ballot: Right to Clean and Healthy Waters 22-02', 22 April 2022, www.floridarighttocleanwater.org/ (accessed May 2025).

10. Alex Howard, 'Florida Right to Clean Water Seeks Floridian Signatures to Preserve Waterways', *NBC2 News*, 21 April 2022, https://nbc-2.com/news/2022/04/21/florida-right-to-clean-water-seeks-floridian-signatures-to-preserve-waterways/amp/ (accessed May 2025).

11. Wesley J. Smith, 'Granting "Rights" to Water, Nature Could Hurt Floridians in Any Number of Ways', *TC Palm*, 23 July 2021, https://eu.tcpalm.com/story/opinion/contributors/2021/07/23/granting-rights-water-could-greatly-hurt-floridians-opinion/8023875002/ (accessed May 2025).

12. Mari Margil, 'Press Release: Orange County, FL, Voters Overwhelmingly Approve "Rights of Nature" Initiative', Center for Democratic and Environmental Rights, 27 April 2021, https://www.centerforenvironmentalrights.org/news/first-us-rights-of-nature-enforcement-case-filed (accessed May 2025).

4 A river with legal personality in Aotearoa/New Zealand

1. Ministry for Culture and Heritage, 'Differences between the Texts of the Treaty of Waitangi', NZHistory, 5 October 2021, https://nzhistory.govt.nz/politics/treaty/read-the-Treaty/differences-between-the-texts (accessed May 2025).

2. Te Awa Tupua (Whanganui River Claims Settlement) Act 2017, Public Act 2017 No. 7.

3. Julia Hollingsworth, 'How Aotearoa/New Zealand's Whanganui River is Legally a Person', *CNN*, 11 December 2020, https://edition.cnn.com/2020/12/11/asia/whanganui-river-new-zealand-intl-hnk-dst/index.html (accessed May 2025).

4. Anne de Vries-Stotijn, Ilon van Ham and Kees Bastmeijer, 'Protection through Property: From Private to River-held Rights', *Water International* 44, nos 6–7 (2019), pp. 736–751.

5. Eleanor Ainge Roy, 'Aotearoa/New Zealand River Granted Same Legal Rights as Human Being', *The Guardian*, 16 March 2017, www.theguardian.com/world/2017/mar/16/new-zealand-river-granted-same-legal-rights-as-human-being (accessed May 2025).

6. See: https://edition.cnn.com/2020/12/11/asia/whanganui-river-new-zealand-intl-hnk-dst

7. Chris Finlayson, 'Internationally Hot, Domestically Not', New Zealand Centre for Global Studies, 3 March 2020, https://nzcgs.org.nz/guest/internationally-hot-domestically-not (accessed May 2025).

8. Laurel Stowell, 'Finally! Upokongaro Cycle Bridge Launched across Whanganui River', *NZ Herald*, 25 March 2020, www.nzherald.co.nz/whanganui-chronicle/news/finally-upokongaro-cycle-bridge-launched-across-whanganui-river/js26502hqzakrdaxwynnt2d2ni/ (accessed May 2025).

5 A difficult struggle for sacred rivers in India

1. NASA, Earth Observations Taken from Shuttle Orbiter Columbia during STS-87 Mission, 1997, PICRYL Public Domain Image, https://garystockbridge617.getarchive.net/amp/media/earth-observations-taken-from-shuttle-orbiter-columbia-during-sts-87-mission-eccd58 (accessed May 2025).

2. National Geographic Society, 'Ganges River Basin', 15 July 2022, https://education.nationalgeographic.org/resource/ganges-river-basin (accessed May 2025).

3. Stuart Butler, 'The Ganges: River of Life, Religion and Pollution', *Geographical Magazine*, 20 January 2022, https://geographical.co.uk/culture/the-ganges-river-of-life-religion-and-pollution (accessed May 2025).

4. National Ganga Rights Act, Ganga Action Parivar, https://gangaaction.org/actions/ganga-rights/ and http://www.gangarights.org (accessed May 2025).

5. Writ Petition (PIL) No. 126 of 2014, *Mohd. Salim vs State of Uttarakhand & Others*, High Court of Uttarakhand at Nainital, 20 March 2017.

6. Reserved Judgment, Writ Petition (PIL) No. 126 of 2014, High Court of Uttarakhand, 12 December 2016.

7. 'Uttarakhand HC Accords Human Status to Ganga, Yamuna', *The Tribune*, 20 March 2017, www.tribuneindia.com/news/

archive/features/uttarakhand-hc-accords-human-status-to-ganga-yamuna-379739 (accessed May 2025).

8. Tawfique Ali, 'Time to Declare Turag Dead', *The Daily Star*, 8 November 2016, www.thedailystar.net/frontpage/time-declare-turag-dead-1310182 (accessed May 2025).

9. Appellate Division of the Supreme Court of Bangladesh, Judgment on Civil Petition for Leave to Appeal No. 3039 of 2019 (17 February 2020).

10. Ashley Westerman, 'Should Rivers Have Same Legal Rights as Humans? A Growing Number of Voices Say Yes', NPR, 3 August 2019.

11. Anima Mundi Law Initiative, 'Rights of Nature Case Study: Turag River', February 2021.

12. Shrishtee Bajpai, '"Righting" the Wrong: Rights of Rivers in India', *Mongabay – India*, 23 June 2020, https://india.mongabay.com/2020/06/commentary-righting-the-wrong-rights-of-rivers-in-india/ (accessed May 2025).

6 The Colombian Amazon rainforest has a right to protection

1. Gabriela Eslava Bejarano, 'Gabriela Eslava Bejarano at Earth Rights Conference 2019', YouTube, 2019, www.youtube.com/watch?v=iafOx6Gd9K8 (accessed May 2025).

2. Dejusticia, '25 Voces contra la Deforestación', 26 April 2018, www.dejusticia.org/25-voces-contra-la-deforestacion/ (accessed May 2025).

3. Dejusticia, 'Tutela Cambio Climático, Tribunal Superior del Distrito Judicial de Bogotá – Sala Civil', 29 January 2018, www.dejusticia.org/wp-content/uploads/2018/01/TutelaCambioClim%C3%A1tico.pdf?x54537&x54537&x54537 (accessed May 2025).

4. See: https://gaiafoundation.org/honouring-thomas-berry-the-founding-father-of-earth-jurisprudence/. See also Thomas Berry, *The Great Work: Our Way into the Future* (New York: Crown Publications, 1999).

5. The Gaia Foundation, 'Principles of Earth Jurisprudence', www.gaiafoundation.org/what-we-do/story-of-origin-

growing-an-earth-jurisprudence-movement/principles-of-earth-jurisprudence/ (accessed May 2025).

6. United Nations, *Report of the Secretary General: Harmony with Nature*, A/75/266, §40, 28 July 2020.

7. César R. Garavito, 'Here Is How Litigation for the Planet Won in Colombia', Dejusticia, 7 May 2018, www.dejusticia.org/en/asi-se-gano-en-colombia-un-litigio-por-el-planeta/ (accessed May 2025).

8. Amazonía Soy, 'Entidades ambientales limitarán la frontera agrícola para cumplir fallo sobre Amazonas', 9 April 2018, https://amazoniasoy.com/entidades-ambientales-limitaran-la-frontera-agricola-para-cumplir-fallo-sobre-amazonas/ (accessed May 2025).

9. Dejusticia, 'Gobierno está incumpliendo las órdenes de la Corte Suprema sobre la protección de la Amazonía Colombiana', 5 April 2019, www.dejusticia.org/gobierno-esta-incumpliendo-las-ordenes-de-la-corte-suprema-sobre-la-proteccion-de-la-amazonia-colombiana/ (accessed May 2025).

10. Dejusticia, 'We Want Zero Deforestation in the Amazon – #LetsStopDeforestation', petition on Change.org, www.change.org/p/presidente-iv%C3%Aín-duque-we-want-zero-deforestation-in-the-amazon-letsstopdeforestation (accessed May 2025).

11. Global Alliance for the Rights of Nature, 'Derechos de la Amazonía', www.garn.org/derechos-de-la-amazonia-2/ (accessed May 2025).

12. Ministerio de Ambiente y Desarrollo Sostenible (Colombia), 'Colombia avanza en la lucha contra la deforestación con una reducción acumulada del 40%', www.minambiente.gov.co/colombia-avanza-en-la-lucha-contra-la-deforestacion-con-una-reduccion-acumulada-del-40/ (accessed May 2025).

7 Rights of Mother Earth in the Constitution of Ecuador

1. Ecuador, Extractive Industries Transparency Initiative, https://eiti.org/countries/ecuador (accessed May 2025).

2. The Carter Center, 'Report on the Constituent Assembly of the Republic of Ecuador', March 2008, www.cartercenter.org/resources/pdfs/news/peace_publications/americas/report6_ecuador_constituent_assembly_march08.pdf (accessed May 2025).

3. Rapid Transition Alliance, 'Buen Vivir: The Rights of Nature in Bolivia and Ecuador', 2 December 2018, www.rapidtransition.org/stories/the-rights-of-nature-in-bolivia-and-ecuador/ (accessed May 2025).

4. Dorine van Norren, *Development as Service: A Happiness, Ubuntu and Buen Vivir Interdisciplinary View of the Sustainable Development Goals*, PhD thesis, Tilburg University, 2017 (Prisma Print, 2017).

5. Carlos Soria, 'Entrevista a Alberto Acosta: Los Derechos de la Naturaleza', *Ecuador Today*, 18 September 2018, https://ecuadortoday.media/2018/09/18/entrevista-a-alberto-acosta-los-derechos-de-la-naturaleza/ (accessed May 2025).

6. Constitución Política de la República del Ecuador, 20 October 2008.

7. Corte Constitucional del Ecuador, Final Judgment (Rights of Nature and Animals as Subjects of Rights), 'Estrellita Monkey' Case, Case No. 253-20-JH, Section 5.1.5.

8. *Ecuarunari and Others v. Ecuacorriente S.A. (ECSA)*, State Attorney General, Ministry of the Environment and Ministry of Natural Resources, Case No. 17111-2013-0317, Provincial Court of Pichincha (20 June 2013).

9. Jeremy Hance, 'Indigenous Leader Murdered before He Could Attend Climate Summit', *Mongabay*, 8 December 2014, https://news.mongabay.com/2014/12/indigenous-leader-murdered-before-he-could-attend-climate-summit (accessed May 2025).

10. Andrés B. Liévano, 'Indigenous Communities Take Legal Action over Ecuador's Largest Mine', *Diálogo Chino*, 4 July 2019, https://dialogochino.net/en/uncategorised/28120-indigenous-communities-take-legal-action-over-ecuadors-largest-mine/ (accessed May 2025).

11. Y. Malhi et al., 'Climate Change and Ecosystems: Threats, Opportunities and Solutions', *Nature Ecology & Evolution* 5

(2021), pp. 1323–1331, www.nature.com/articles/s41559-021-01450-y.epdf (accessed May 2025).

12. Ana C. Basantes, 'Mining Company Pressing to Enter Ecuador's Los Cedros Protected Forest', *Mongabay*, 22 May 2020, https://news.mongabay.com/2020/05/mining-company-pressing-to-enter-ecuadors-los-cedros-protected-forest/ (accessed May 2025).

13. Gustavo Prieto, 'The Los Cedros Forest Has Rights', *Verfassungsblog*, 10 December 2021, https://verfassungsblog.de/the-los-cedros-forest-has-rights/ (accessed May 2025).

14. MOTH (More-Than-Human Life program), 'Song of the Cedars', 28 October 2024, https://mothrights.org/2024/10/28/song-of-the-cedars/ (accessed June 2025).

15. Museum for the United Nations – UN Live, 'Sounds Right – Nature Is the New Artist', April 2024, www.museumfortheunitednations.com/sounds-right (accessed June 2025).

16. Craig M. Kauffman and Pamela L. Martin, 'Can Rights of Nature Make Development More Sustainable? Why Some Ecuadorian Lawsuits Succeed and Others Fail', *World Development* 92 (2017), Appendix Table I.

17. Down to Earth Staff, 'Chile Poised to Grant Rights to Nature: Could Become 2nd Such Country besides Ecuador', *Down to Earth*, 31 March 2022, www.downtoearth.org.in/news/environment/chile-poised-to-grant-rights-to-nature-could-become-2nd-such-country-besides-ecuador-82168 (accessed May 2025).

18. Laura Burgers, 'Klimaatzaken: De rol van de rechter en een ontwikkeling in het recht', *Klimaatweb*, 1 September 2021, https://klimaatweb.nl/nieuws/klimaatzaken-de-rol-van-de-rechter-en-een-ontwikkeling-in-het-recht/ (accessed May 2025).

8 Spain is leading the way in Europe with rights for a lagoon

1. PETI Committee, Fact-finding Visit to Mar Menor, Spain, 23–25 February 2022, briefing, European Parliament, https://www.europarl.europa.eu/cmsdata/245205/BRIEFING.pdf (accessed May 2025).

2. Miguel Angel Ruiz, 'El Caballito del Mar Menor, Casi Desaparecido', Asociación Hippocampus, 20 December 2017,

www.asociacionhippocampus.com/noticias/el-caballito-del-mar-menor-casi-desaparecido/ (accessed May 2025).

3. Heather Galloway, 'The Race to Make Spain's Mar Menor a Legal Person', *El País in English*, 4 August 2021, https://english.elpais.com/society/2021-08-04/the-race-to-make-spains-mar-menor-a-legal-person.html (accessed May 2025).

4. Murcia Today, 'Over 70,000 People Attend Mar Menor Protest Demonstration in Murcia', 8 October 2021, https://murciatoday.com/archived-_-over-70000-people-attend-mar-menor-protest-demonstration-in-murcia_1660377-a.html (accessed May 2025).

5. *Spanish News Today*, 'Spanish MPs Vote to Give Mar Menor Lagoon Personhood and Rights', 6 April 2022, https://spanishnewstoday.com/spanish-mps-vote-to-give-mar-menor-lagoon-personhood-and-rights_1759340-a.html (accessed May 2025).

6. Carolijn Terwindt and Jessica den Outer, 'Legal Personality for the Mar Menor Lagoon in Spain', Embassy of the North Sea, 2022, www.embassyofthenorthsea.com/legal-personality-for-the-mar-menor-lagoon-in-spain/ (accessed May 2025).

7. Ley 19/2022, de 30 de septiembre, para el reconocimiento de personalidad jurídica a la laguna del Mar Menor y su cuenca, *Boletín Oficial del Estado*, 3 October 2022.

8. Eduardo Salazar Ortuno, 'La Ley que Reconoce Derechos al Mar Menor y su Cuenca: Un Nuevo Paradigma para la Defensa Jurídica de la Naturaleza', *Abogacía Española*, 26 September 2022, www.abogacia.es/publicaciones/blogs/blog-derecho-ambiental/la-ley-que-reconoce-derechos-al-mar-menor-y-su-cuenca-un-nuevo-paradigma-para-la-defensa-juridica-de-la-naturaleza/ (accessed June 2025).

9 Love Our Ouse: campaigning for river rights in England

1. Greg Dickinson, 'England's Underrated River that's Become the Cleanest in the Country', *The Telegraph*, 3 March 2023, www.telegraph.co.uk/travel/destinations/europe/united-kingdom/england/east-sussex/why-englands-underrated-river-become-cleanest/ (accessed 5 May 2025).

2. The Rivers Trust, *State of Our Rivers Report*, 2024, https://theriverstrust.org/key-issues/state-of-our-rivers#:~:text=No%20single%20stretch%20of%20river,every%20stretch%20of%20English%20rivers (accessed May 2025).

3. UK Climate Risk (CCRA3), *Evidence Report: England Summary*, 2021, www.ukclimaterisk.org/wp-content/uploads/2021/06/CCRA-Evidence-Report-England-Summary-Final.pdf (accessed May 2025).

4. RiverRights.org, 'Groups', www.riverrights.org/groups.html (accessed 5 May 2025).

5. Love Our Ouse, official website, https://loveourouse.org/ (accessed 5 May 2025).

6. Love Our Ouse, 'Charter for the River Ouse', 2025, https://loveourouse.org/wp-content/uploads/2025/03/Charter-for-the-River-Ouse-1.pdf (accessed May 2025).

7. See:https://loveourouse.org/wp-content/uploads/2025/02/Press-Release-Rights-of-River-Charter-for-the-River-Ouse-1.pdf

8. Lasserina Rath, 'Rights of Rivers: Victory in the UK – The Journey, Challenges, and Implications' (12 December 2023), *Impakter*, https://impakter.com/rights-of-rivers-victory-in-the-uk-the-journey-challenges-and-implications/ (accessed 5 May 2025).

10 Nothing is more powerful than an idea whose time has come

1. Earth4All and Global Commons Alliance, *Global Commons Survey 2024: Public Attitudes Across the World on Planetary Stewardship*, conducted by Ipsos, April 2024, https://res.cloudinary.com/dfyeeawiq/images/v1724426386/Global-Commons-Survey-2024-Global/Global-Commons-Survey-2024-Global.pdf (accessed May 2025).

Further reading

General Rights of Nature

Alex Putzer, Tineke Lambooy, Ronald Jeurissen, and Eunsu Kim, 'Putting the Rights of Nature on the Map: A Quantitative Analysis of Rights of Nature Initiatives across the World', *Journal of Maps* 18, no. 1 (2022), pp. 89–96.

Earth Law Center, www.earthlawcenter.org (accessed May 2025).

Eco Jurisprudence Monitor, https://ecojurisprudence.org/ (accessed May 2025).

Center for Democratic and Environmental Rights, www.center forenvironmentalrights.org/ (accessed May 2025).

Community Environmental Legal Defense Fund, https://celdf.org/ (accessed May 2025).

Laura Burgers and Jessica den Outer, *Compendium Rights of Nature: Case-studies from Six Continents* (Ambassade van de Noordzee, 2021).

Global Alliance for the Rights of Nature, www.garn.org (accessed May 2025).

UN Harmony with Nature, 'Rights of Nature Law and Policy', available at www.harmonywithnatureun.org/rightsOfNature/ (accessed May 2025).

Michelle Nijhuis, 'Rights for Rivers: Fighting for the Legal Rights of Nature', *Yes!* (6 July 2021) www.yesmagazine.org/environment/ 2021/07/06/rights-of-nature-conservation (last accessed May 2025).

Miranda Willems, Tineke Lambooy, and Setara Begum, 'New Governance Ways Aimed at Protecting Nature for Future Generations: The Cases of Bangladesh, India and Aotearoa/New Zealand: Granting Legal Personhood to Rivers', *IOP Conference Series: Earth and Environmental Science* 690 (2021).

3 Water bodies appear before judges in Florida

Elizabeth Kolbert, 'A Lake in Florida Suing to Protect Itself', *The New Yorker*, 18 April 2022), www.newyorker.com/magazine/2022/04/18/a-lake-in-florida-suing-to-protect-itself (accessed May 2025).

Isabella Kaminski, 'Streams and Lakes Have Rights, a U.S. County Decided. Now They're Suing Florida', *The Guardian*, 1 May 2021), www.theguardian.com/environment/2021/may/01/florida-rights-of-nature-lawsuit-waterways-housing-development (accessed May 2025).

Katie Surma, 'Two Lakes, Two Streams and a Marsh Filed a Lawsuit in Florida to Stop a Developer From Filling in Wetlands: A Judge Just Threw It Out of Court', *Inside Climate News*, 7 July 2022), https://insideclimatenews.org/news/07072022/two-lakes-two-streams-and-a-marsh-filed-a-lawsuit-in-florida-to-stop-a-developer-from-filling-in-wetlands-a-judge-just-threw-it-out-of-court/ (last accessed May 2025).

4 A river with legal personality in Aotearoa/New Zealand

Domenico Amirante and Silvia Bagni (eds), *Environmental Constitutionalism in the Anthropocene: Values, Principles and Actions* (London: Routledge, 2022), Part II, Chapter 3.

Miriama Cribb, Elizabeth Macpherson, and Axel Borchgrevink, 'Beyond legal personhood for the Whanganui River: collaboration and pluralism in implementing the *Te Awa Tupua Act*', *International Journal of Human Rights*, 16 February 2024.

Moana Ellis, 'Gerrard Albert: Why Whanganui River Tribes Have Moved beyond Co-governance to a New Model for Better Democracy', *NZ Herald*, 11 April 2022), www.nzherald.co.nz/whanganui-chronicle/news/gerrard-albert-why-whanganui-river-tribes-have-moved-beyond-co-governance-to-a-new-model-for-better-democracy/us3pvhbyw2ftkugmo7abp5zw4e/ (accessed May 2025).

New Zealand Parliament, 'Innovative Bill Protects Whanganui River with Legal Personhood', 28 March 2017, www.parliament.nz/en/

get-involved/features/innovative-bill-protects-whanganui-river-with-legal-personhood/ (accessed May 2025).

Radio New Zealand, 'New Strategy for Wellbeing of Whanganui River to Be Unveiled', 27 September 2023, www.rnz.co.nz/news/national/498002/new-strategy-for-wellbeing-of-whanganui-river-to-be-unveiled (accessed May 2025).

5 A difficult struggle for sacred rivers in India

Outlook Web Bureau, 'Supreme Court Stays Uttarakhand HC Order Declaring Ganga, Yamuna a "Living Entity"', *Outlook India*, 7 July 2017, www.outlookindia.com/website/story/supreme-court-stays-uttarakhand-hc-order-declaring-ganga-yamuna-a-living-entity/299507 (accessed May 2025).

Sheetal Sharma, 'Ganga and Yamuna as a Living Entity: What Does This Mean to the Rivers?', *Legal Service India*, www.legalserviceindia.com/legal/article-8146-ganga-and-yamuna-as-a-living-entity-what-does-this-mean-to-the-rivers-.html (accessed May 2025).

6 The Colombian Amazon rainforest has a right to protection

Advancing Child Rights Strategic Litigation, 'Colombia Supreme Court, Sentencia STC 4360-2018, Radicación No. 11001-22-03-000-2018-00319-01', www.acrisl.org/casenotes/mudzuru-ampamp-another-v-ministry-of-justice-legal-ampamp-parliamentary-affairs-no-ampampothers-const-application-no-7914-cc-12-15-2015-zwcc-12-20-january2016ccz-122015-ghfkj-b44w5-wz5en-mwjha (accessed May 2025).

Dejusticia, 'In Historic Ruling, Colombian Court Protects Youth Suing the National Government for Failing to Curb Deforestation', 5 April 2018, www.dejusticia.org/en/en-fallo-historico-corte-suprema-concede-tutela-de-cambio-climatico-y-generaciones-futuras/ (accessed May 2025).

Demanda Generaciones Futuras v. Minambiente, 2018, overview of related rulings, http://climatecasechart.com/non-us-case/

future-generation-v-ministry-environment-others/ (accessed May 2025).

Mariana E. Roldán, 'Eight Key Points of the First Latin American Lawsuit on the Rights of Future Generations and Climate Change', Dejusticia, 29 January 2018, www.dejusticia.org/en/eight-key-points-first-latin-american-lawsuit-rights-future-generations-climate-change/ (accessed May 2025).

7 Rights of Mother Earth in the Constitution of Ecuador

Alberto Acosta, 'Embedding Pachamama in the Constitution', *The Green Interview* (January 2014), https://thegreeninterview.com/interview/acosta-alberto/ (accessed May 2025).

Natalia Greene, 'The First Successful Case of the Rights of Nature Implementation in Ecuador', Global Alliance for the Rights of Nature (21 May 2011), www.garn.org/first-ron-case-ecuador/ (last accessed May 2025).

Global Alliance for the Rights of Nature, 'The Case for Rights of Nature in Face of the Mirador Open Pit Copper Mining Project', 26 February 2013, www.garn.org/the-case-for-rights-of-nature-in-face-of-the-mirador-open-pit-copper-mining-project/ (accessed May 2025).

María E. Merino, 'How Ecuador's Courts Are Giving Form and Force to Rights of Nature Norms', *Transnational Environmental Law*, 12, no. 2: 366–395. www.cambridge.org/core/journals/transnational-environmental-law/article/abs/how-ecuadors-courts-are-giving-form-and-force-to-rights-of-nature-norms/186BBD0B99125ED2BAB3FE752C386FEA (accessed May 2025).

8 Spain is leading the way in Europe with rights for a lagoon

Simon Hunter, 'Some 250 Kilos of Dead Fish Wash up in Murcia's Mar Menor', *El País in English* (18 August 2021), https://english.elpais.com/society/2021-08-18/some-250-kilos-of-dead-fish-wash-up-in-murcias-mar-menor.html (last accessed May 2025).

The Spain Journal, 'Vox Criticizes the Unworthy Witch Hunt of the Progressive Consensus Against Farmers', 16 December 2020,

https://web.archive.org/web/20210119000851/https://
thespainjournal.com/vox-criticizes-the-unworthy-witch-hunt-of-
the-progressive-consensus-against-farmers/ (accessed May 2025).

9 Love Our Ouse: campaigning for river rights in England

Environmental Law Foundation, 'Historic Decision Sees River Ouse
Set to Become First in England with Legal Rights', https://elflaw.
org/news/historic-decision-sees-river-ouse-set-to-become-first-
in-england-with-legal-rights/ (accessed 5 May 2025).

Lewes District Council, 'Council Champions Pioneering Rights of
River Charter to Protect Landmark Waterway', www.lewes-
eastbourne.gov.uk/article/3167/Council-champions-pioneering-
Rights-of-River-Charter-to-protect-landmark-waterway (last
accessed 5 May 2025).

Lewes District Council, 'Rights of Rivers: A Charter for the River
Ouse – Lead Member Decision Notice', https://democracy.lewes-
eastbourne.gov.uk/documents/s34505/Lead%20Member%20
Decision%20Notice%20-%20Rights%20of%20Rivers%20A%20
Charter%20for%20the%20River%20Ouse.pdf (last accessed 5 May
2025).

Index

The Pluto Press Newsletter

Hello friend of Pluto!

Want to stay on top of the best radical books we publish?

Then sign up to be the first to hear about our new books, as well as special events, podcasts and videos.

You'll also get 50% off your first order with us when you sign up.

Come and join us!

Go to bit.ly/PlutoNewsletter